1.8.80

The Origins of the Gospel Traditions

The Swedish scholar Birger Gerhardsson departs from the form-critical approaches and directs biblical investigation to the pre-history of the written gospels. He carefully examines the origins and history of the gospel traditions from the lifetime of Jesus to the appearance of the written gospels.

Gerhardsson's viewpoint is that the primary setting for the early Christian transmission of the Jesus tradition is tradition itself. This tradition must be understood as a conscious, technical art of instruction. Acknowledging the creative character of early Christian interpretations, Gerhardsson upholds that "it is one thing to take these changes in the transmitted material in all seriousness, and quite another thing to presume that the early church freely constructed the Jesus traditions, placed the words of early Christian prophets and teachers in Jesus' mouth, and so on."

The Origins of the Gospel Traditions presents a Scandinavian alternative to classical continental form-criticism in biblical studies. It provides students of the Bible with a summary of a significant perspective not previously available in English.

The Origins
of the
Gospel Traditions

BIRGER GERHARDSSON

FORTRESS PRESS   PHILADELPHIA

This book is a translation of *Evangeliernas Förhistoria* (Lund: Verbum-Håkan Ohlssons Förlag, 1977), copyright © 1977 by Birger Gerhardsson.

Biblical quotations from the Revised Standard Version of the Bible, copyright 1946, 1952, © 1971, 1973 by the Division of Christian Education of the National Council of the Churches of Christ in the U.S.A., are used by permission.

ENGLISH TRANSLATION COPYRIGHT © 1979 by FORTRESS PRESS

Library of Congress Cataloging in Publication Data

Gerhardsson, Birger.
  The origins of the Gospel traditions.

  Translation of Evangeliernas förhistoria.
  Lectures given in March 1976 at Holzhausen, Ger.
  Bibliography: p.
  1. Bible. N. T. Gospels—Criticism, interpretation, etc.—Addresses, essays, lectures. I. Title.
BS2555.2.G4413   220.6   78-19634
ISBN 0-8006-0543-8

7416J78   Printed in the United States of America   1-543

Contents

Introduction

Research has expended enormous effort and great ingenuity in order to enable us, if at all possible, to work out the historical truth about Jesus of Nazareth. Do our sources—and above all the first three Gospels—provide us with a somewhat dependable picture of Jesus: who he was, what he proclaimed, what he did, and what form his fate took?

During the nineteenth century scholars worked with these questions primarily in the literary-critical manner. They sought to get a firm hold on the oldest information in the Gospels by getting at the *literary sources* the evangelists had built upon. Gradually, however, they began to see that this would not produce the desired results, for it is obvious that there was a period of *oral tradition* which lay between Jesus' ministry and the earliest written records. What had happened to these remembrances during this preliterary period?

A bold step forward was taken in this area in the years right after World War I. This effort came to be known as the "form-critical school," and its pioneers included Martin Dibelius *(Die Formgeschichte des Evangeliums,* 1919*), Rudolf Bultmann *(Die Geschichte der synoptischen Tradi-*

**From Tradition to Gospel,* trans. Bertram Lee Wolfe (New York: Charles Scribner's Sons, 1934).

tion, 1921*), and Karl Ludwig Schmidt (*Der Rahmen der Geschichte Jesu*†). Using insights which had been provided initially by researchers of antiquity, folklore specialists, and Old Testament exegetes, these scholars sought to clarify the oral tradition in the early church. They sorted out the Gospel material into types of forms *(Gattungen),* and sought to place these into the context in which they were thought to have appeared and been used in the activity of the early church (i.e., the materials' *Sitz im Leben*). These men further wrote the history of these traditions and set forth judgments concerning their historical value. Bultmann in particular showed great skepticism here. The results had a great effect on Gospel research in Germany, and in other countries too the scientific study of the Gospels was influenced more than by any other scholarly findings in the past fifty years. And this has happened even though much of the work of this "form-critical school" has been hotly debated.

This is not the place to provide a closer look at the presuppositions, methods, and results of the "form-critical school." What I intend to do here is to present a brief description of how I, for my part, look upon the question of the Gospel tradition's origin and history from the time of Jesus to the appearance of the written Gospels.

My chief objection to the form-critical scholars—whom I agree with in part, but in part decidedly differ from—is that their work is not sufficiently *historical.* They do not show sufficient energy in anchoring the question of the origin of the Gospel tradition within the framework of the question how holy, authoritative tradition was transmitted in the

---

**History of the Synoptic Tradition,* trans. John Marsh, based on the 3d German edition (New York: Harper & Row, 1963).
   †(Berlin: Trowitzsch & Sohn, 1919.)

Jewish milieu of Palestine and elsewhere at the time of the New Testament. This must surely be the starting point if one wants to understand the origins of the early Christian tradition historically.

The subject of this book is therefore the origins of the Gospel material and the history of its transmission, or, in other words, the prehistory of the written Gospels (especially the Synoptics). I shall approach the problem as one would in secular historiography. Theological viewpoints will be suggested only in passing. To prevent misunderstandings I should, however, say that an investigation of the origins of the Gospels with the methods of secular history can certainly produce important results for New Testament theology, but at the same time one cannot base theology on these results directly. New Testament theology must reasonably begin with a consideration of *the Christian faith's original meaning and content,* not with questions regarding the origins of the basic source material. On the other hand, historical questions cannot be answered by theological argumentation.

This book consists of a series of lectures presented in March 1976 to German theological students at Holzhausen, outside of Marburg. That explains why I have not found it necessary to define in more detail the form-critical viewpoint which I accept in part and reject in part, nor the exegetical-historical background in general. This also explains why I have not taken up a number of preliminary questions of scientific and historical nature, questions one certainly cannot ignore in dealing with problems of this kind. Other lecturers dealt with these matters at Holzhausen.

Finally, the lecture form also explains why I so seldom identify sources and literary references. For support of my position I would refer the reader to two of my books,

Memory and Manuscript: Oral Tradition and Written Transmission in Rabbinic Judaism and Early Christianity* and *Tradition and Transmission in Early Christianity.*† Both books contain ample references to source materials as well as scholarly literature. I might also point out that in both of these youthful works I often quite deliberately expressed myself a bit pointedly. Furthermore, I would call attention to the list of works in the bibliography of this book.

---

*2d ed. (Uppsala and Lund: C. W. K. Gleerup, 1961, 1964).
†(Lund: C. W. K. Gleerup, 1964.)

1

Jewish Traditionalism

Discovery and research in the last generations have made it clear to us that Judaism in Palestine at the beginning of our era was much less homogeneous than was previously known. Many disparate tendencies and group formations existed. They did not all think alike. Nonetheless, it is proper to speak of "Judaism" as a characteristic entity and to point to certain qualities which united the different Jewish groups and tendencies. One must naturally draw a line somewhere. I do not, for example, include those Jews who had gone so far in the direction of assimilation to the surrounding culture that they no longer had their sons circumcised.

One characteristic which united all Jewish groups was the conviction that Israel was God's chosen people, a people to whom it had pleased God to give a special standing among the nations by entering into a covenant with them. Because this covenant had been entered in the past, had been made between God and the people's ancestors, the terms of the covenant existed as *tradition*. At the beginning of our era monotheism was firmly established among the Jews. Other gods held little attraction. The Jews maintained that they were in covenant with the one true God; the God of their fathers was for them the one true God. They sought for no new, radical revelations to replace the old. What they wanted to know was how the inherited divine revelation was to be understood in the here and now. There were of course groups that were drawn to new signs and revelations—apocalyptic and prophetical groups—but even these did not want to break with the old. It was typical, for example, that the Qumran community expected that the new revelations would be found *in* Torah, that is, in the ancient Holy Scriptures.

That binding religious inheritance from the fathers, which served as a source of inspiration and a binding norm for both communal and individual life, was identified by the inclusive term *Torah*. This word *Torah,* which we usually render "the Law," actually has a much broader content than this would suggest. It points to the entire revelation and instruction which Israel's God has given to his people. All pious groups in Israel wished to be faithful to Torah. They might have varied opinions about Torah's character and content and scope, but all were united in their pride and joy in Torah, and in their recognition of its binding nature as a norm for living. It has been said that Judaism had become *Torah-centric* (William Farmer).

For the dominant element of Jewish society, the Pharisaic-rabbinical element, Torah included Israel's national, binding cultural inheritance in its entirety. One could suggest a pedagogical simplification and say that Torah functioned in three external forms or dimensions: (1) as verbal tradition, (2) as practical tradition, and (3) as institutional tradition.

By *verbal* tradition I refer to words and texts, either as written in books or imprinted on the mind (or both), that is, written and oral tradition. By *practical* tradition I refer to inherited, binding patterns of living: normative conduct impressed upon the people by those in positions of authority through deeds and through verbal instruction, conduct which was learned by imitation and listening. By *institutional* tradition I refer to the institutions and establishments that generation after generation supported, for example, the Temple and the synagogues, or such objects as the inscriptions on the doorposts, phylacteries, tassels on cloaks, and so on.

Much could be said about this comprehensive and highly diversified tradition which in its wholeness possesses religious authority, and about its varied components, as well as about its transmission from generation to generation. But I must limit myself to certain aspects presented in a brief and sketchy form.

How did it happen that this traditionalism grew so strongly in Israel in the centuries around the beginning of our era? I have already suggested that the embryo of Jewish traditionalism is to be found in the covenant concept itself. In the reports of how God enters into a covenant with father Abraham we note that this covenant is not only to involve him but also his "seed," his descendants. He is to direct his children and his "house" to hold to God's way and to live justly and righteously (Gen. 18:19). And in the description of how this covenant is consummated at Sinai we note the same thing. The generation of Israelites then living is obligated to make known to its children and grandchildren all that the covenant includes (Deut. 4:8ff.; 6:4ff.).

During the exile the Jews' religious and national uniqueness was threatened. Such threats served to make the national inheritance more precious, and its maintenance an even greater concern (cf. e.g., Ezra 7:10, 21-26). This development reached its zenith a couple of hundred years later. After Alexander the Great's victory at Issos (333 B.C.), Hellenistic culture infiltrated Palestine and was accepted by many Jewish families.* When Palestine came under Seleucid domination (198 B.C.) this tendency increased. The climax was reached when the Seleucid king, Antiochus Epiphanes, abetted the process of Hellenization with threats and violence (167 B.C.). He attempted, by decree and by threats of extreme sanctions, to use his power to Hellenize Judaism in its entirety: politically, culturally, and religiously.

There were of course a number of Jews who gave in to these royal threats. But others reacted in a different spirit to the foreign despot. Their identity, their distinctive character, was threatened at the core. An intense opposition came to life. Loyalty to that which was "Jewish" flamed up. For the Jews who became involved in this reaction all things native and inherited became holy and binding: not only the fathers' faith and ethos, but all else that their fathers had maintained: the Law, the customs, the institutions. The land and the language of their fathers, indeed all things Jewish, had to be defended at all costs. "Zeal" (in Greek, *zēlos*) for all such now became an ideal. The books of the Maccabees give us an eloquent description of the situation.

It is highly possible that the term *Judaism* (in Greek, *joudaismos*) was coined in this very context as the opposite of *Hellenism* (in Greek, *hellēnismos*). The word *joudaismos* first appears in 2 Maccabees (2:21; 8:1; 14:38).

Some Jews took up arms in order to protect their holy heritage. Others carried on a spiritual war, a religious cultural struggle. In both instances men strove earnestly for their fathers' God and his Torah; their zeal simply took different forms.

*See Martin Hengel, *Judentum und Hellenismus,* 2d ed. rev. (Tübingen: J. C. B. Mohr, 1973), pp. 120–52. English trans.: *Judaism and Hellenism,* 2 vols. (Philadelphia: Fortress Press, 1974). Cf. also Hengel, *Juden, Griechen und Barbaren* (Stuttgart: KBW Verlag, 1976).

2

Master and Disciples

It was during this cultural struggle that Jewish traditionalism, with its unbending opposition to all forms of adaptation and assimilation, began to take on its uncompromising quality. And it was within the context of this development that the ancient Jewish school system took shape. In the Greek world the schools were an effective means of spreading and establishing Hellenistic culture. If we can believe the books of the Maccabees, there were Hellenistic schools in Palestine during the second century before Christ; there was even a Hellenistic "gymnasium" for young men in Jerusalem itself (cf. 1 Macc. 1:14; 2 Macc. 4:9). It was about that time that the Jews began to set up their own schools in an effort to steel their youth against the blandishments of Hellenism. These Jewish schools were similar in some respects to the Hellenistic schools, but their purpose was different. They were designed above all to convey to their young the pure inheritance of the ancient Jewish fathers, and to form (or socialize) them into true Israelites, faithful to the traditions and life-style of the fathers. There was really but one subject in the curriculum, but that one subject included everything: Torah.

In this picture of a Torah-centric Judaism we also see that it is markedly *patriarchal*. "The fathers" play a leading role as authorities and teachers. That is true both of the family fathers in the individual "houses" as well as of the fathers of the people, "the elders," that is, the persons of honor. The leading men were always of a respectable age, and it was these who acted as the authoritative representatives of the heritage of the fathers.

Among these persons of honor are some who are especially significant: these are the *experts* of various kinds, those who, because they have grown up in a certain set of circumstances or have received a special training, are experts in certain facets of the inherited tradition. For example, there are those who have mastered the texts of the Holy Writings, and who now gather the young around them in schools of various sizes. The priests are another example; they have learned from older, more knowledgeable priests through many years of service in the Temple, and as a result have become experts themselves in carrying out the various aspects of the Temple ministry. Then too, there are those who have become specialists in the application of the Law. There are also teachers of wisdom of different kinds, the successors of the makers of proverbs in ancient Israel, closely related to the popular philosophers in the Hellenistic culture. Such men as these now stood out as significant *witnesses* to the ancient heritage; they were now able to *testify* to the wisdom and the way of life of the fathers. We can also mention here prophetical figures and workers of miracles. The distinction between prophets and teachers was rather nebulous in the ancient world. Prophets too had their disciples, the "sons of the prophets." In the intertestamental literature, in the historical writings of Josephus, in the New Testament, and above all in the rabbinical literature, we meet these various Torah authorities, surrounded by their disciples and supporters.

Inasmuch as knowledge is something imparted, it must be sought where it can be found. To learn Torah one must go to a teacher. Where else can one go? Students flock around their teachers. And such a group formation—teachers and their students—becomes something of an extended family. The teacher is the spiritual father, the students his spiritual children. They spend their time with him, they follow him ("walk after" him, in Hebrew, *hālak achare*), they serve him. The house where he dwells, whether it is in fact his own or belongs to a patron, is also their house. It has been pointed out properly enough that the leading schools of the New Testament period are highly concrete realities. "Hillel's house" and "Shammai's house" are designations which refer not only to sizable spiritual families, but also to the very buildings where they met together.

Students learn much of the Torah tradition by *listening:* by listening to their teacher and his more advanced students as well as by posing questions and making contributions of their own within the bounds prescribed by modesty and etiquette. But they also learn a great deal by simply *observing:* with attentive eyes they observe all that the teacher does and then proceed to imitate him. Torah is above all a holy, authoritative attitude toward life and way of life. Because this is true, much can be learned simply by watching and imitating those who are learned.

In the Talmud, that miscellany of material collected from discussions held in the rabbinical schools, we can see how the participants quote what various teachers have said. Some one has heard rabbi so-and-so say this or that. But we also note here references to what the learned men actually have done: "I saw rabbi so-and-so do thus and so." The rabbinical tradition preserves examples of how bright and eager students followed their teachers' actions even in the most private situations, motivated by the belief that "This has to do with Torah, and I want to learn!" A humorous story tells how two students one evening hid themselves in their teacher's bed-room where he slept with his wife. When the teacher suddenly discovered them he was naturally angry, but they defended themselves by arguing in all innocence that this too involved Torah, and they wanted to learn.

Such examples indicate to us that the person involved learns not simply the texts and the obligatory way of life cultivated in a certain school, but also the spirit and atmosphere created by a teacher and his students working together in their community. It is interesting to note how certain visible and audible characteristics come to identify those who belong to a certain school. Certain peculiarities in their conduct, or certain manners of speaking, suffice to indicate that an individual belongs to "Hillel's school" or to "Shammai's school," or whatever. The initiated observer can thus tell from such externals to what school a person learned in Torah belongs.

Against this background it is easy to see why it was that the traditions collected by the rabbis not only include pronouncements but also stories.

3

Oral Transmission

During the first four centuries of our era the oral Torah tradition of the Jewish rabbis grew enormously. And it was still being handed down orally. If one wonders how it was possible for such a huge body of text material to be preserved and passed on orally, one must consider the rabbis' pedagogical methods and the technique employed in oral transmission. I shall here provide a brief sketch of certain typical aspects of their oral instruction. The oldest specific evidence dates as a rule from the years following the fall of the Temple (A.D. 70) and the destruction of Jerusalem (A.D. 135). But in essential aspects these methods are clearly ancient:

(1) I would emphasize first of all the fundamental role of *memorization.* We forget all too easily that this is a very old pedagogical technique. Before the art of writing became common, memorization was the only way of preserving a statement or a text. And this primitive method proved to be very tenacious. Among Jewish teachers in antiquity we note that virtually all important knowledge was learned in the form of sayings and texts which were imprinted on the memory, so that one knew them by heart. (This method is by no means extinct in the Orient. Just recently a colleague—a Swedish professor of medicine—reported that he had lectured in Egypt. After his first lecture, a number of students

came forward to ask if he could not summarize the major points in such a way that they could be memorized. The mechanical memory has not been rejected in pedagogics all over the world!) It must also be remembered that memorization is not some sophisticated academic speciality but rather a decidedly *popular* means of retaining information.

(2) A teaching pattern which shows up time after time is that of *text and commentary*. Methodical study divides itself into two elements: (*a*) the learning of the text, and (*b*) the effort required to comprehend the meaning of the text: analysis, commentary, exposition. *Learning* a text and *understanding* it are, as we all know, two different matters, differing as memory does from intelligence. A written text must be produced before it can be commented upon. The same is true of oral tradition. First of all, an oral text must be, as it were, written on the student's memory; only then can the exegesis begin.

(3) It is important that teachers speak tersely and incisively. They must avoid wordiness and vacuity in speech. If they wish to impress their wisdom upon the memories of their students, they must express themselves in concise terms. The rabbis used to say that one must always instruct in the briefest way possible (in Hebrew, *derek qesārāh*). For many centuries the teachers of wisdom in Israel cultivated the art of curbing their tongues. "Let your words be few," said the Preacher (Eccles. 5:2), for example, and he was certainly thinking not only of prayer and conversation, but also of teaching. The rabbis kept up this tradition. "A sharp peppercorn is better than a basket full of cucumbers," they said.

(4) These teachers also made use of various *didactic and poetic devices*. For example, they used picturesque or pointed formulations, alliteration and assonance, rhythmic phrases,

parallelismus membrorum, symmetrical arrangement of phrases, a verbatim repetition of introductory phrases, and so on. Such poetical devices were not of course utilized only to make statements easier to remember, but in practice they also served that purpose. It is easier to remember poetry than prose, rhythmic sentences than nonrhythmic, the picturesque than the pedestrian, the well-organized than the unorganized.

(5) *Repetition* is, in this context, self-evident and natural. The old Romans used to say that repetition is the mother of all knowledge. Ancient Jewish pedagogy was in complete agreement. The teachers would repeat their main points word by word, several times, and the students would then reiterate those same points over and over until they knew them by heart. Written texts were learned in the same manner: they were drilled into the students until they were memorized. Knowledge thus acquired was then retained by diligent, word-for-word repetition. In the rabbinical writings we often see a picture of the ideal scholar. He never sits idle in his house, but he sits there repeating and meditating. He never goes about absentminded or filled with worldly thoughts. He recites and meditates while he is going. The admonitions found in Deut. 6:6–7 no doubt formed the ideal: "And these words which I command you this day shall be upon your heart; and you shall teach them diligently to your children, and shall talk of them when you sit in your house, and when you walk by the way, and when you lie down, and when you rise" (cf. also Josh. 1:8 and Ps. 1:1–2).

(6) When the texts were read and repeated, this was done not in an ordinary, conversational tone, but rhythmically and melodiously, as a *recitation.* The words were half sung. In antiquity reading was done aloud. The same held true for oral repetition. Only certain secret instructions were whispered.

Thus we see that in the transmission of the texts the very sound of the words and the rhythm and melody of the sentences play an interesting role.

(7) Many teachers and students also utilized the *art of writing* as an aid in the preservation of important instruction and tradition. Most of the Jewish teachers in the centuries from the birth of Christ and onward were able to write. But it is still hard to determine the role that writing may have played in their teaching and oral transmission. According to tradition, the Pharisaic-rabbinical movement in Judaism maintained a distinction between written Torah and oral Torah, and deliberately propagated the view that oral Torah is to be handed down verbally and not in book form. But whether or not this principle was already recognized in Jesus' time is a subject of debate. The unusually prolific Jewish-American author Jacob Neusner published in 1971 a sizable work entitled *The Rabbinic Traditions about the Pharisees before 70.** This is in many respects a most helpful study. Neusner here works through many of the same questions I dealt with in my dissertation *Memory and Manuscript.* I must of course lament the caricaturelike way he presents my book and summarizes my positions. Neusner's work does, however, have its Achilles' heel. He has accepted in an uncritical fashion as his main thesis an idea of his teacher Morton Smith, and sets out consciously to substantiate it.† The Smith thesis is that there is no real evidence which enables us to determine the tradition methods utilized in the early Christian congregations or by the Pharisees prior to A.D. 70. According to Smith and Neusner the memorizing technique we see used by the

---

*3 vols. (Leiden: E. J. Brill, 1971).
†See Smith's negative review of my *Memory and Manuscript,* in *Journal of Biblical Literature* 82 (1963): 169–76.

rabbis was a radical novelty, introduced by the rabbinical schools during the second century A.D. This novelty also included the rule that oral Torah was to be handed down verbally, with no help from books. I am not at all convinced that Neusner is justified in reaching the final conclusion that we know nothing of how the Pharisees preserved their traditions prior to A.D. 70. After eliminating statements and evidence found in the rabbinical literature, in Josephus, and in the New Testament, Neusner can only assert that the rabbis introduced a radically new methodology after the fall of the Temple, and speculate as to why this occurred.

I still maintain that the Pharisees and their scribes distinguished between written and oral Torah already in New Testament times, and that they did not accept any official books containing oral Torah. But—and this is the point here—this did not prevent them from making *private memoranda* of material found in the oral tradition. In other words, a distinction was made between official books and private memoranda. In the rabbinical tradition we can glimpse records of various kinds: "scrolls of secrets," notebooks, and other memoranda. Such probably appeared among the students of Hillel and Shammai as early as Jesus' time. Private notations of this kind were found above all in the schools of the Hellenistic world, where they were referred to as *hypomnēmata, apomnēmoneumata, chreiai,* and so on.

I would add parenthetically that we are still waiting for a solid dissertation which, on the basis of a careful investigation of written notes of this kind in the Hellenistic schools, would enable us to determine the role such memoranda played among Jesus' disciples and among the teachers and traditionists of the early church. In 1946 an all-too-brief but stimulating book dealing with such problems was published posthumously. The author was the learned English provost R. O. P. Taylor, and the book was entitled *The Groundwork of the Gospels.** This work has not received the attention it deserves. It should also be mentioned that in the past few years a clear tendency to emphasize strongly the role of *written* transmission in early Christianity has appeared, particularly among American scholars. Some even go so far as to deny that the Jesus tradition ever existed as a purely oral tradition. How far one can carry this train of thought is still an open question.†

(8) The rabbis were not much interested in studies limited to mere cramming and mechanical recitation. They were very conscious of the importance of comprehending and personally applying that which had been impressed upon one's mind. For this reason they carried on an energetic *struggle against lifeless knowledge.* They criticized with both humor and irony those who had memorized great masses of textual material without understanding what their own mouths were saying. They compared such persons to magicians who mumble formulas which they do not understand, or to lifeless baskets filled with scrolls. According to the rabbis a disciple ought not be a dead receptacle for the received tradition. He should rather enter into it so that he understands it and is in agreement with it. Only thus can he actually live according to it, be a fruitful steward of it, and pass it on to others in an infectious way. A living bearer of the tradition is to be like a torch which has been lit by an older torch, in order that it might itself light others.

---

*(Oxford: Blackwell, 1946.)

†As a guide to this discussion I refer the reader to E. Earl Ellis, "New Directions in Form Criticism," in *Jesus Christus in Historie und Theologie, Festschrift* in honor of H. Conzelmann (Tübingen: J. C. B. Mohr, 1975), pp. 299–315.

4

Allusions to the Torah Tradition in the New Testament

In Acts 22:3 Luke has Paul, then in custody, speak as follows to a crowd in Jerusalem: "I am a Jew, born at Tarsus in Cilicia, but brought up in this city at the feet of Gamaliel, educated according to the strict manner of the law of our fathers, being zealous (*zēlōtēs*) for God as you all are this day."

Luke's Paul here summarizes the comprehensive norm-system by which he has been brought up and educated within the Jewish community with the words: "the law of our fathers" (*ho patrōos nomos*). This same Paul, in Acts 28:17, uses the comprehensive designation: "the customs of our fathers" (*ta ethē ta patrōa*). It is also of interest to note that (in Acts 22:3, quoted above) he mentions by name his chief teacher, Gamaliel.

In Gal. 1:14 Paul himself speaks of his youth: "I advanced in Judaism (*joudaismos*) beyond many of my own age among my people, so extremely zealous was I for the traditions of my fathers (*hai patrikai mou paradoseis*)." With these words the apostle refers to the authoritative tradition which the leading teachers of the Jewish people in the New Testament times preserved and set forth.

The very same Jewish tradition is also mentioned in the synoptic Gospels. Particularly helpful for our purposes here is the pericope dealing with mealtime customs in Mark 7 and Matthew 15. Here we see references to "the tradition of the elders" (Mark 7:3, 5; Matt. 15:2), a tradition which "the Pharisees and all Jews" (Mark), "the scribes and the Pharisees" (Matthew) uphold in addition to "God's commandments" in the sacred Scriptures. Other terms from the Jewish tradition of a technical or quasi-technical nature also appear: "to pass on" (as tradition, *paradidonai,* Mark 7:13); "to receive" (as tradition, *paralambanein,* Mark 7:4); "to keep" the tradition (*tērein,* Mark 7:9); "to maintain" the tradition (*kratein,* Mark 7:3, 8); "to uphold" the tradition (*histanai,* Mark 7:9 var.); "to walk according to" the tradition (*peripatein kata,* Mark 7:5); "to transgress" the tradition (*parabainein,* Matt. 15:2).

Thus Paul and the evangelists are conscious of the fact that the Jews of their time have a tradition—incorporating many traditions—which they scrupulously maintain. The phrases they use indicate that this tradition is not accepted by all of the people, but also that it is of concern for others besides Pharisees. It is referred to as "the tradition of the fathers" or "the tradition of the elders," and the Pharisees and their scribes are understood to be its most influential representatives. The Jewish historian Josephus also indicates that the Pharisees had a dominant position among the people.

5

Tradition in Early
Christianity

If we bear in mind that Paul of Tarsus was reared in this
Jewish tradition, as it was upheld and observed and handed
down by the Pharisaic scribes, it is of real interest to proceed
to the writings of this same Paul as a Christian apostle. In
these writings he speaks of the early church's own tradition.
It will be worth our while to take note of the manner in which
he speaks of this.*

According to Paul, the church possesses a normative
standard which he refers to as "tradition" or "traditions"
(*paradosis, paradoseis,* 1 Cor. 11:2; 2 Thess. 2:15; 3:6). The
manner in which this is passed on is expressed in the verbs
paradidonai, "hand over" (tradition), and *paralambanein,*
"receive" (as tradition), 1 Cor. 11:23; 15:1, 3; Gal. 1:9; Phil.
4:9; 1 Thess. 2:13; 4:1; 2 Thess. 3:6. The young Christian
congregations are to "maintain" or "hold fast to," or
"uphold" these traditions; the verbs used here are, among
others, *kratein* (2 Thess. 2:15), *katechein* (1 Cor. 11:2), and
hestēkenai (1 Cor. 15:1). We also have the expression "to
walk according to" such traditions (*peripatein kata,* 2 Thess.
3:6). In the deutero-Pauline pastoral Epistles we find such

*See Oscar Cullmann, *Die Tradition als exegetisches, historisches und theolog-
isches Problem* (Zürich: Zwingli-Verlag, 1954), pp. 12–16. English trans. in *The
Early Church* (London: SCM Press, 1956), pp. 54–99, 62–66.

terms as *tērein* and *phylassein,* which mean "to keep," "to observe," "to hold" (1 Tim. 5:21, 6:14, 20; 2 Tim. 1:14).

On the basis of terminological agreement of this nature it is of course not possible to draw the simple conclusion that early Christianity possessed a tradition of precisely the same kind as did the Jews. Early Christianity was, as we well know, critical of the Jewish tradition and revolted against it. But we are entitled to establish one thing: in Paul's time early Christianity is conscious of the fact that it has *a tradition* of its own—including many *traditions*—which the church leaders hand on to the congregations, which the congregations receive, and which they then are to guard and live after. In Paul's time there exists a *conscious, deliberate,* and *programmatic* transmission in the early church.

One observation ought perhaps to be included here. The pioneers in the form-critical school were of the opinion that the early church, in its very first phase of development, was not disposed to pass on a tradition: it lacked that perspective on the future which is necessary if one is to see any reason for doing so. This indicates that the form-critical school had a one-sided understanding of transmission as taking place only from one generation to the next. In both the Jewish and the early Christian sources, however, we can see that tradition is not merely something that happens between generations. Transmission also occurs within one and the same generation when binding material is passed on. Whenever authoritative material is passed on to someone who receives it, a form of transmission has taken place.

6

Paul as a Bearer of Tradition

In several places in his letters, Paul tells us that he has passed on and that he passes on tradition—Christian tradition—to his congregations. What kind of a picture do we see in the Pauline Epistles of the apostle functioning in this role?

We who belong to the Lutheran branch of the Christian church ought—if any—to be conscious of how radically and spiritedly Paul speaks about freedom "in Christ," about the church's freedom, about the freedom of the individual Christian. For those who have been added to the body of Christ through baptism all things are free, everything is permitted, all is pure. Everything belongs to them. Their conduct of life is and must be a "walk in the Spirit." And "where the Spirit of the Lord is, there is freedom" (2 Cor. 3:17). Paul is therefore the last one to want to place upon his congregations some kind of "yoke of bondage," an obligatory system of norms complete with commandments and decrees and rules.

It is precisely because he held such a view that it is of so great interest to note how Paul nevertheless speaks of the existence of a normative tradition and normative traditions within the church. Here a brief reminder will suffice of how Paul describes himself in his role as a bearer of tradition.

Paul looks upon himself as a spiritual father to those who have been won for the gospel (1 Cor. 4:17; Philem. 10), and the congregations he has founded (1 Cor. 4:14ff.; 2 Cor. 12:14; Gal. 4:19; 1 Thess. 2:11). And he admonishes his congregations to be imitators (*mimētai*) of him in all respects, even as he himself is an imitator of Christ (1 Cor. 4:16; 11:1; 1 Thess. 1:6; 2 Thess. 3:7).

What the apostle has in mind when he speaks of imitating Christ and imitating Paul is naturally in the final analysis a great mystery, a fruit-bearing unity in the Spirit between the heavenly Lord and his true followers in the world. But Paul also thinks quite concretely of the life of imitation which comes into being when obedient disciples receive, and pattern their lives according to, the instruction of their teacher. We note for example that the admonition in 1 Cor. 4:16, "Be imitators of me," is followed immediately by the concrete statement: "Therefore I sent to you Timothy, my beloved and faithful child in the Lord, to remind you of my ways in Christ, as I teach them everywhere in every church" (1 Cor. 4:17). When Paul speaks of "my ways" he is referring to patterns of his life and teachings. *Imitatio Pauli* (imitating Paul) means, in large measure, the same as to receive and live according to the teaching which Paul proclaimed in all of his congregations. This involves, in the first place, instruction in words, both orally and in writing. In 2 Thess. 2:15 the apostle writes to the congregation in Thessalonica: "So then, brethren, stand firm and hold to the traditions which you were taught by us, either by word of mouth or by letter." In Phil. 4:9 we note further that Paul does not think only of the tradition which he passes on in articulated form—as words, spoken or written—but also of what he does and arranges. He says: "What you have learned and received [from me] and heard and seen in me, do." That tradition is not meant only for the individual can be seen in such passages as Phil. 3:17:

"Brethren, join in imitating me, and mark those who so live as you have an example in us."

These texts should be commented upon from various points of view, but I shall content myself with three observations:

(1) The pneumatic, charismatic character of early Christianity does not exclude authoritative tradition and a conscious transmission. Even though Paul radically espouses the freedom of the Christian to "walk in the Spirit" in the presence of God, he nonetheless deliberately passes on tradition and traditions to his congregations, and requests them to accept them and live according to them.

(2) It is clear in Paul that the traditions are not intended only for individuals, but that they are given to the congregations to be upheld within the context of the Christian fellowship. The traditions belong to the common life of the early Christian congregations. To this extent the assumptions of the form-critical school are supported by the material. But the fact is that Paul does not speak of the traditions as though they are the wind of the Spirit, or profound driving forces or tendencies which work anonymously in the congregations, spreading wildly from place to place. The transmission of tradition is first of all associated with the work of leading men of authority of various kinds. The example provided in 1 Cor. 4:16f. is particularly clear. The normative tradition has come to the congregation directly from Paul, and it is brought to completion by Paul's disciple, Timothy—the apostle's spiritual son—who comes to the congregation in order to instruct them further concerning the "ways," that is, the teachings and the way of life which Paul customarily impresses on all of his congregations.

(3) We must also note that the tradition has different

dimensions. The fact that Paul passes on tradition—and traditions—to his congregations means that he imparts to them a faith, a spirit, a confession, a proclamation, an instruction with an inner power scarcely accessible for analysis, but which nonetheless took place through external forms, of which we can catch a glimpse behind his descriptions. We can see most clearly the *verbal* dimension of the tradition he provided (oral and written), and quite clearly too of the *practical* dimension (a model way of life, a model pattern for "how you ought to live and to please God," words taken from another passage, 1 Thess. 4:1). But we also sense here the *institutional* dimension of the Pauline tradition: forms of organization that will enable the congregation to function (e.g. 1 Cor. 11:34b; 14:26–40).

7

Paul and the Jesus Tradition

Now we shall pose the next question: In the diversified tradition which he passed on to his congregations, did Paul also include traditions about Jesus, what he had said and done during his earthly life? In other words, Did Paul include that which we customarily refer to as "gospel tradition" or "Jesus tradition"?

Many scholars are of the opinion that Paul neither wanted to know anything about Jesus' earthly activity nor did he actually know anything significant about it. For a number of exegetes this is such an obvious fact and so cherished a belief that they can only smile at any attempt to ascertain what Paul could have known of Jesus' words and deeds. I find this an amazing position.

It is certain that Paul does not quote the earthly Jesus very often in his Epistles, nor does he discuss such material. But neither are his Epistles entirely free of direct quotations from the Jesus tradition. Furthermore, he repeats in his Epistles time after time that he already has handed down an authoritative tradition to his congregations (e.g., 1 Cor. 11:2, 23; 15:1ff.; Gal. 1:9; Phil. 4:9; 1 Thess. 2:13; 4:1; 2 Thess. 2:15; 3:6), and he makes references to that which his hearers have already heard or already have knowledge of (e.g., Phil. 4:9; 1 Thess. 2:13; 2 Thess. 2:15). We further note that Paul often develops his argumentation on the basis of certain premises which he assumes are shared by his readers. It seems to me to be a highly legitimate historical task to attempt to answer such questions as these: What was the nature of the authoritative tradition material which Paul had passed on to his congregations before he wrote his Epistles to them? And did this material include "gospel tradition"?

Time does not permit us to discuss here the entire question concerning the extent of Paul's knowledge of the Jesus tradition as revealed in his Epistles, how much he takes for granted and hints at in his presentations. I shall be content to touch briefly upon a few passages in which he clearly *adduces* the Jesus tradition, and two passages where he quotes directly.

The apostle writes in 1 Cor. 7:10: "To the married I give charge, not I but the Lord, that the wife should not separate from her husband." In verse 12 he continues as follows: "To the rest I say, not the Lord, that if any brother has a wife who is an unbeliever, and she consents to live with him, he should not divorce her." And further on (in v. 25) he asserts: "Now concerning the unmarried, I have no command of the Lord, but I give my opinion as one who by the Lord's mercy is trustworthy." Here Paul is providing instruction in a context of *halakah*; he is providing authoritative guidance for the Christian congregation in questions regarding marriage. And in the process of doing so he makes reference to the words of Jesus (cf. Matt. 5:32; 19:9). He does not quote word for word, but expresses the *intent* of the words while he himself formulates the terse regulations. We also note that Paul—in the manner of a rabbi—clearly indicates the authority which stands behind the rules in question. He makes a clear distinction between his own words and those of the Lord. Finally, we observe how Paul proceeds when he does not have a specific word from Jesus to support him. He then states without circumlocution that in such cases he cannot refer to any command of the Lord, but is simply providing his own opinion. These passages are embarrassing evidence against the common opinion that in the early church no distinction was made between what was said "by the Lord (himself)" and what was said by some one else "in the Lord"; that words of Jesus were freely constructed, or that sayings of some early Christian prophet were freely placed in the mouth of Jesus. In 1 Corinthians 7 we see how such a man as Paul, at least on occasion, very clearly upheld the distinction between that which was said "by the Lord" and that which was said "in the Lord."

In 1 Cor. 9:14 the apostle writes: "In the same way, the Lord commanded that those who proclaim the gospel should get their living by the gospel." In this passage Paul does not quote the words of Jesus, but himself formulates the *halakah*-type statement that one may draw from them (cf. Matt. 10:9f.; Luke 10:7). Here Paul presupposes the words of Jesus.

Another instance in which Paul appears to be quoting directly from the sayings of Jesus is found in 1 Thess. 4:15. The question here touched upon is not halakic, but eschatological or apocalyptic. Paul writes: "For this we declare to you by the word of the Lord [*en logō Kyriou*], that we who are alive, who are left until the coming of the Lord, shall not precede those who have fallen asleep." It seems probable here that Paul is referring directly to a transmitted saying of Jesus. But he does not quote this saying directly in this instance either; he is simply expressing in his own words the answer which he has extracted from the saying of Jesus regarding this question.

We must now leave such texts and turn to the two passages in which Paul expressly *quotes* gospel tradition. These are found in 1 Cor. 11:23ff.; and 15:1ff. In both instances the text which has been handed down is introduced with a formula which indicates that the apostle is quoting directly. 1 Cor. 11:23 begins as follows: "For I received [*paralambanein*] from the Lord what I also delivered [*paradidonai*] to you, that . . ." In 15:3 we read: "For I delivered to you first of all what I also received, how that . . ."

The tradition text quoted by the apostle in the first instance (1 Cor. 11:23ff.) is the account of Jesus' Last Supper. The wording is not Paul's, but is traditional. The version which is quoted is the one which (in a later form) was also written down by Luke (22:19f.; cf. the par.). If we scrutinize the apostle's line of thought, we note that he is here concerned to build upon the actual words of Jesus in the text, that the bread is "my body" and the cup is "the new covenant in my blood." This is undoubtedly the reason why Paul says that he has received this from the Lord (*apo tou Kyriou*). The idea is then that the Lord spoke these words to the disciples who were present on the occasion of the Last Supper, and that these men subsequently passed the tradition on.

The other tradition text (1 Cor. 15:3ff.) includes a brief summary of the decisive events in the Jesus' story: "that Christ died for our sins in accordance with the scriptures, that he was buried, that he was raised on the third day in accordance with the scriptures, and that he appeared to Cephas, then to the twelve," and so on. Paul does not here name the person who passed this text on to him; he simply says that he received it as tradition. But we note here both in the quotation formula he uses as well as in the non-Pauline wording employed in the quoted text, that he is repeating a traditional text.

It is clear from these passages that Paul is aware of a way of handing on the Jesus tradition in the form of direct quotation; in other words, he knows how to transmit a text which has been formulated in a fixed manner. And if we ask ourselves what it is that this old rabbinical student has in mind when he says that he has "delivered" to the congregation words which he himself has "received," it seems that we have hardly more than two possibilities to choose between. Either the apostle has passed the text on in a written form which the congregation then has at its disposal, or he has presented the text orally, and impressed it upon them in such a way that the congregation (or more precisely, one or more of its leaders) knows it by heart. To "hand over" a text is not the same as to recite it once. It rather means that the text is presented to the hearers in such a way that they have "received" it and possess it. For my own part I find it easiest to assume that Paul is referring here to an *oral* transmission.

By drawing on a number of Pauline texts, I have pointed out that the apostle obviously was well-acquainted with a variety of ways of transmitting tradition. The two passages we have just considered (1 Cor. 11:23ff. and 15:1ff.) reveal to us (I can interpret this in no other way) that Paul also was familiar with and utilized a simple, direct *transmitting of texts,* when that was necessary; that is, he quite simply passed on a text to a recipient, either in writing or orally. In the latter case the text was *taught* to the recipient in such a way that he knew it by heart. It was written upon his mind. This was a complete activity in itself, not a component part of an ongoing process of proclamation or instruction.

Perhaps I should say a word about how I came upon this idea. It happened in the year 1955/56 when I was occupied with a licentiate dissertation on the Epistle of James. As is well known, Martin Dibelius has written the most influential commentary on this epistle.* In his opinion, James is a typical product of early Christian parenesis ("exhortation"). Dibelius believes that the sayings of Jesus in the Synoptic tradition had their primary *Sitz im Leben* in early Christian parenesis; it was there that they were passed on. The Epistle of James is full of allusions to the sayings of Jesus, most of these from the Sermon on the Mount. But as I studied these allusions, it came to me that the words of Jesus in the synoptic Gospels cannot have had their primary *Sitz im Leben* in early Christian parenesis. It seems completely clear that those involved in parenesis were not inclined to make quotations. Such exhortations are generally delivered in a traditional manner; they are full of borrowed motifs, ideas, words, and phrases. They reflect little originality on the part of the speaker. But those who admonish intend to do so themselves, on their own authority, and not to quote others. We even find that quotations from the sacred Scriptures are few and far between in parenesis. The Scriptures are alluded to, motifs and formulations are derived from them, but they are almost never quoted. The same is true of the relationship of parenesis to the oral tradition. In parenesis men speak in a traditional style, using borrowed raw material; but they do the speaking themselves, they do not quote. They are not dis-

Brief des Jakobus (Göttingen: Vandenhoeck & Ruprecht, 1921).

posed to pass on specific words received from others. For this reason the Sermon on the Mount and the Epistle of James do not come from the same *Sitz im Leben.* By the same token, *Pirke Avot* ("The Sayings of the Fathers") does not come from the same *Sitz im Leben* as the parenetic parts of Jewish literature. There is a distinct difference between collections of traditional sayings and the like, and parenetic admonitions. They comprise two different forms (*Gattungen*) for presenting material.

Dibelius is, in part, quite clear about this. He takes the position that early Christianity handed down the sayings of Jesus in two ways: in parenetic contexts, and in collections which contained exclusively sayings of Jesus, which the missionaries took with them either in oral or written form.* But for Dibelius, the former way was the primary one. For my part, I cannot see how parenesis has any claim at all to be the *Sitz im Leben* for the words of Jesus. The Jesus traditions were a part of the traditional material which one merely *alluded to* and *built upon* in parenesis.

I suspect, on the other hand, that Paul has provided us with a dependable clue by quoting in two passages texts which he expressly designates as verbal tradition. Here we sense the primary *Sitz im Leben* for the early Christian transmission of Jesus tradition; this is, paradoxical though it may seem, transmission itself, transmission as a conscious, technical act of instruction.

Before leaving this theme I must make a number of observations:

(1) In 1 Cor. 11:23ff. and 15:1ff. Paul is not specifically *handing down* the two texts which he quotes. He is not pro-

From Tradition to Gospel, p. 242.

viding a new Jesus tradition for the congregation. He is simply repeating two traditions which he explicitly says he already has delivered to the congregation. If we suppose that the congregation in Corinth had understood and held fast to the instruction Paul had previously provided concerning the Lord's Supper and his death and resurrection, then Paul really would have had no reason to repeat these two traditions in his letter; he had already passed them on to the congregation. But in that case we would have known even less about that which he delivered to his congregations prior to the time he wrote to them. That is worth thinking about.

(2) In spite of the fact that Paul repeats traditional texts which he has received from others, he feels free to insert interpretative elements into them, to make clarifying additions to such texts. The parenthetical remark that Paul makes in 1 Cor. 15:6 ("most of whom are still alive, though some have fallen asleep") is certainly an addition which the apostle makes to the text he has received. Then too, we cannot be certain where his direct quotation in 1 Cor. 15:3ff. ends. This may be because the apostle in this instance does not intend to pass on a traditional text in authentic form for the first time to his readers, but simply repeats a text which the congregation has already received in an authentic form. But I doubt that this explanation is the whole story. We see in the synoptic Gospels that the Jesus tradition has been reworked during the period of its transmission in the early church, that abridgments and additions have been made in an effort to make the meaning clearer. So it is not without interest to note that Paul here in 1 Corinthians 15 has made certain small interpretative alterations of the text. We shall return to this later on.

(3) The text which Paul repeats in 1 Corinthians 15 is a particularly significant one, for this is a summary of the basic kerygma, listing the decisive events surrounding the death and resurrection of Jesus. But even so, not all of the traditions which he points to here by using brief association-words (e.g., "he appeared to Cephas, then to the twelve") have been preserved in the synoptic Gospels. Particularly amazing is the loss of the tradition concerning the appearance of the resurrected Jesus to Cephas, the fundamental, first appearance of the resurrected One (unless a fragment of this has been preserved in Matt. 16:18f.). Also without a trace are the traditions about the appearance of the resurrected Jesus to more than five hundred brethren at one time, and the appearance to James. This serves as a reminder that we cannot simply equate the Jesus traditions passed on by Paul to his congregations at their inception with any one of our synoptic Gospels, or all three together. It will not do, therefore, to think of our Gospels as copies of a complete and mechanically unaltered recording of Jesus' teaching and of the firsthand reports of eyewitnesses.

8

Early Christianity and the Past

The apostles, evangelists, and teachers of early Christianity wanted to address the people of their day, to speak to their listeners about something of concern to them. Naturally they were not concerned to provide documentation and archives for dead memories from the past. I can go along with Martin Dibelius to this extent, when he elegantly describes how early Christianity lived in the present and in an intensively longed-for future.

But the whole argument is distorted if one forgets that early Christianity nonetheless had a genuine interest in the past, and a natural feeling for the fact that ancestors and generations before no longer live here on earth, as well as for the fact that God's activities have their appointed times, irrevocably following one after the other. Furthermore, early Christianity had a special reason for being interested in one specific aspect of the past: that which concerned Jesus of Nazareth, who, after an outstanding ministry, was crucified by Pontius Pilate, and then arose from the dead.

None of the evangelists intends to write about a dead man's final destiny. All of them write about a person whom they understand to be alive today, a celestial Lord to whom they daily turn in prayer and other acts of worship. But they write about his work in Israel during an era which lies in the past. It is not true to say that they give free, concrete expression to their present faith in the heavenly Lord, and to their answers "in Christ's Spirit" to contemporary questions, by creating myths about what he says to the congregations today. Not even John, whose desire to permit Jesus' divine splendor to shine through in his words and deeds has strongly influenced the style of the Fourth Gospel, writes simply about the present for the present. He is conscious of a chronological, spatial, and factual distance between himself and Jesus' activity in Galilee and Judea. He writes of a time when "the Spirit had not yet been given," "when Jesus was not yet glorified," when Jesus had not yet been "lifted up from the earth" so that he might "draw all men [even the heathen] to himself," a time when the disciples "did not yet understand," inasmuch as the Spirit of truth had not yet come to "guide them into all truth"—to use a few of John's own formulations (7:39; 12:16, 32; 16:13, cf. also 2:22).

We see in the Synoptics even more clearly than in John how the evangelists and their sources look back to an era which lies in the past, and which is separated from the present, not only chronologically but also spatially and factually. It is admittedly true that this perspective has been broken through or toned down in various places—the splendor of the resurrection has colored the traditions—but this in no way detracts from the general impression that the intent of the evangelists is to describe the ministry of Jesus in Israel up to and including his death and resurrection in Jerusalem. It is a ministry which leads forward to the exalted position Jesus has in the present, but this goal is not reached until the final chapter.

For my part, I find the way Jesus' closest followers are described in the Gospels well worth considering. When the evangelists write, Peter, James, and John, indeed all of "the Twelve," are men of reputation in the church. They are spoken of with reverence, and their spirit and power are the subject of stories. In Acts 5:15 Luke reports the popular legend about Peter which claimed that he could heal the sick merely by passing by them so that his shadow fell upon them. That is indicative of the high opinion men had of Peter at the time the evangelists wrote. But when the evangelists come to write about Jesus' earthly activity in Galilee and Jerusalem, Peter and James and John and the other disciples are not presented as a group of spiritual heroes, but as men conspicuously weak, immature, lacking in knowledge and understanding. This is not the situation in the church after Easter but the situation during Jesus' earthly ministry. But it does show that the early Christians preserved memories of the past, and sensed the distance between themselves and the past. There is a tendency in the tradition—we see it in Matthew, Luke, and John—as time went on to tone down the negative presentation of Jesus' closest disciples in the older texts, but this tendency merely serves to confirm our observation. Herbert Braun says in his book *Jesus** that there is also a tendency in the Gospel tradition to depict the disciples worse and worse, but he provides no proof of this tendency, nor can it be proved.

This characteristic looking backward in time is found in the Gospels, but perhaps it is not found in the tradition's oldest form. Could it be that we are dealing with a secondary historicizing? Jürgen Roloff has posed this question in his book *Das Kerygma und der irdische Jesus,*† and he demonstrates

---

Jesus: Der Mann aus Nazareth und seine Zeit (Stuttgart: Kreuz-Verlag, 1969), p. 48. English trans.: *Jesus of Nazareth: The Man and His Time,* trans. Everett R. Kalin (Philadelphia: Fortress Press, 1979).

†(Göttingen: Vandenhoeck & Ruprecht, 1970.)

that this was not the case. Even in the layers which are usually looked upon as the oldest, we can see that early Christianity was conscious of the distance between itself and that which occurred during Jesus' earthly ministry. Roloff provides a number of examples which indicate that the situation as described in the Gospel tradition does not at all reflect the circumstances in the church after Easter, and he shows that Jesus' activity prior to the crucifixion is described in the Gospel tradition as a veiled appearance, limited in space, without success, and tied to conditions which presuppose his time and situation. The early church has tried to understand these past events better, has interpreted them, has even permitted its interpretations to affect the material. But the early Christians preserved the memory of a distinct segment of past history and feel their dependence on it. Thus the problems of the young Christian congregations have *colored* the material, but not *created* it. This looking back upon Jesus' earthly ministry is an essential factor in the early Christian tradition formation right from the very beginning.

9

The Concentration on "The Only Teacher"

The primary characteristic of all of the books in the New Testament is undoubtedly the central role played in them by the person of Jesus Christ. This is especially obvious in the four Gospels. They were written exclusively in order to present Jesus. Other people of course appear in them too: Jesus has his followers; he soon has his bitter opponents; the masses respond to his activity, first receptively, only to turn against him later. The disciples, the opponents, and the masses all play distinctive roles, and as a rule the evangelists describe them with great care. But the spotlight is always on Jesus. The purpose of the Gospels is to describe him and no one else: *his* appearance in Israel, what *he* said, what *he* did, what happened to *him*. It is true that there are traditions which deal with John the Baptist, but this is the case simply because his fate becomes intertwined with that of Jesus.

It is worthy of notice that the evangelists give Jesus' closest disciples quite insignificant roles in what happens; I have already touched on this. During the decades between the departure of Jesus and the appearance of the Gospels, men such as Peter and James and John certainly said many things that might have been considered worthy of being recorded and given to the congregations. But never for a moment do the evangelists yield to the temptation to supplement what

Jesus has to say with a speech of Peter or James or John. Their intention is to present Jesus and no one else.

Matthew quotes Jesus as saying: "For you have [only] one teacher [*didaskalos*], and you are all brethren" (23:8). This saying is presumably secondary (an interpretation), but it nevertheless gives expression to an attitude which all four of the evangelists seem to have shared. They are concerned exclusively with what Jesus has said to God's congregation (and done for it). I shall return later to the question how those with such a concern nonetheless seem to feel free to rework the tradition and to reformulate some of the sayings of Jesus.

The extraordinary concentration upon Jesus becomes particularly obvious when the Gospels are compared with the literature of Jewish tradition. Many teachers appear in the latter; the Talmud refers to nearly two thousand rabbis by name. They are all held in esteem, they are quoted with respect. But here interest is centered on Torah, not on any individual rabbi. Statements made by different rabbis are placed side by side; the authority of one differs from that of another only by degree. That is not the case in the Gospels. One figure—Jesus—stands in a class by himself, enjoying a unique authority. Whenever he appears, he dominates the scene in a sovereign manner. No one even approaches his stature.

If one thinks about it, it becomes extremely difficult to imagine that there ever was a time when Jesus' followers were not interested in preserving his teachings and in committing his deeds to memory. And if we orient ourselves historically, and remind ourselves how students in the Jewish milieu hung on the words of their teachers and attentively followed their activities in order to learn how to live properly, it then becomes difficult to believe that Jesus' disciples could have been less concerned to hear their master, to observe his way of doing things, and to store up all of this in their memories.

As the Gospels also reveal, this concentration upon Jesus in regard to content is matched by a formal concentration upon Jesus. The evangelists are conscious theologians; this is clear from the way they design their work, group their material, form connecting notices, omit formulations, add formulations, alter formulations. But they do not see it as their task to write a reasoned presentation of Jesus, setting forth his message and doctrines in their own words mixed in with theological comments, doctrinal argumentation, or hortatory speeches. They permit Jesus to speak for himself, as a rule in direct discourse. They report episodes involving Jesus tersely and to the point. They do not allow themselves to comment—except for occasional, concise, and scarcely noticeable remarks in links between pericopes. This is very conspicuous when the Gospels are compared to the other books in the New Testament. We shall return to this later.

10

Continuity in the View of Jesus

This concentration upon Jesus—the *isolation* of the Jesus tradition—has not escaped the attention of Rudolf Bultmann. With a reference to Gerhard Kittel, he emphasizes this prominent characteristic in the early Christian collections of Gospel traditions.* But according to Bultmann, the first evangelist (Mark) is so far removed from the earthly Jesus that he can only hear the whisper of his voice. Two wide and deep chasms separate Mark from the Jesus who was crucified by Pontius Pilate: that between Jesus and the original Palestinian congregation after Easter, and that between this early Palestinian Christianity and early Hellenistic Christianity.

Bultmann contends that Jesus' activity was entirely non-messianic. To the extent that material in the traditions show characteristics which may be classified as messianic, it must be judged as secondary. The conditions necessary for the rise of the Jesus tradition did not exist until after Easter. It is true that many Jesus traditions appear in the early Palestinian congregation: people remembered him, gathered information, even added Jesus traditions of their own making. Collections of such traditions also began to appear. But these collections were merely "enumerations and summings up"

*Rudolf Bultmann, *The History of the Synoptic Tradition,* 2d ed. (Forest Grove, Oreg.: International Scholarly Book Services, 1968), pp. 368f.

(*Aufreihungen, Summierungen*). In early Palestinian Christianity there was lacking the dominant concept around which the Jesus traditions could have been organized into a coherent unity: the myth about the crucified and risen Lord. This myth had its origins in the Hellenistic congregation, and was given form in the Hellenistic congregation's basic message (kerygma). And thus it was that Mark was able to produce the first coherent Gospel: he used this myth and this kerygma as his point of departure.

It is difficult today to go along with Bultmann's train of thought. And it just is not true that it is based simply upon a detailed analysis of the traditional Gospel material, free of all presuppositions. This train of thought is also built upon a priori presuppositions:

(1) When one labels all of the so-called messianic characteristics in the Gospel traditions "secondary," that is based in large measure on the view one has of what Jesus was like and of what the early Christian kerygma amounted to.

(2) When it is asserted that tradition formation could have begun only after Easter, that is based not least of all on the manner in which one envisions a tradition-building community. Heinz Schürmann has shown in a famous essay (*Die vorösterlichen Anfänge der Logientradition**) that the sociological conditions required for the appearance of Gospel tradition must have been present in the community which gathered around the earthly Jesus.

(3) When one makes a clear distinction between Palestinian and Hellenistic Christianity, one is building upon a clear-cut

---

*Published in H. Ristow and K. Matthiae, eds., *Der historische Jesus und der kerygmatische Christus,* 2d ed., (Berlin: Evangelische Verlagsanstalt, 1961), pp. 342-70. Reprinted in *Traditionsgeschichtliche Untersuchungen zu den synoptischen Evangelien* (Düsseldorf: Patmos-Verlag, 1968), pp. 37-65.

distinction between "Palestinian" and "Hellenistic" which is not possible to draw today. We now know that Hellenistic culture had gained a secure footing on Palestinian soil even before Jesus' time—even among the Aramaic-speaking Jews.

These are complicated questions, but I am going to attempt to describe my primary objection very briefly. I contend that the material shows an obvious continuity in the Jesus tradition, a continuity which reveals itself not least of all at its very heart, in the view of Jesus.

In those layers of the Gospel tradition which are generally considered the oldest, Jesus already appears with an overwhelming authority (*exousia*). He preaches and teaches about the reign of God, he heals the sick and expels demons in a remarkable manner. It is also typical that he concentrates on rescuing the socially and religiously downtrodden. Jesus does not say much about himself, but he conducts himself with supreme authority, and his disciples treat him with unreserved veneration and devotion. The amazement of the masses is a part of this picture too. In my judgment, there is a rather straight line which proceeds from this situation to the situation after Easter, when early Christianity worships Jesus as the Messiah, God's Son, the Lord (*Kyrios*). A development has taken place—a many-sided, complicated development— above all because of what has happened to Jesus, but also because the faith of his followers has been strengthened and developed. But there is a fundamental continuity to be seen in the exclusive and dominant position Jesus occupies in the eyes of his disciples. In an engrossing study entitled *The Mission and Achievement of Jesus,** Reginald H. Fuller has put it that the "raw material" for the high Christology of the

*(London: SCM Press, 1954.)

early church is already present in the traditions from Jesus' earthly ministry. That, I believe, is a quite appropriate way of describing the situation.

Let me provide three examples:

(1) From what we know of the use of titles in Palestine at the beginning of our era, we have every reason to believe that from the very first day of his public manifestation in Israel Jesus was addressed as "Lord" ("my Lord," "our Lord"; in Aramaic, *māri, māran,* or *māranā;* in Greek, *Kyrie*). It was thus that honored persons were addressed. It seems that this title has remained a part of the Jesus tradition all the way, only gaining in potency, steadily acquiring greater weight and significance. The title was appropriate the whole time, while Jesus' authoritative teaching and mighty deeds elevated him in the eyes of his followers and at last placed him at the right hand of power as "King of kings and Lord of lords," with a lordly name that coincides with "the name that is above all other names." This development was advanced significantly by the Easter event, with the certainty that Jesus had been exalted after his suffering. But it would be hard to prove that a radically new trend began at that point, and even harder to say that this new trend appeared first of all in the Hellenistic branch of early Christianity. I do not believe that the title Lord (*Kyrios*) can be used to demonstrate that there was a break in the development of the Jesus tradition.

(2) A similar continuity can be seen in the *Son of God* Christology. The idea that Israel is "God's son" was cherished in the Old Testament and in the later Jewish tradition, and the king of Israel is called God's son, for example, in the Psalter (2:7). In the fragmentary Midrash to 2 Samuel 7 found at Qumran (4Q flor. 1:10–13), we note that this title could be used in reference to the coming

Messiah as well. And in the intertestamental literature (Sirach, the Wisdom of Solomon) as in the rabbinical writings, we have evidence that this idea could be democratized and individualized and used to refer to "righteous" individuals in Israel. In the New Testament material we find that the young church after Easter designates Jesus as God's Son in a special sense; he stands over all others and has a unique right to call God his Father. The older formulations, for example, in Rom. 1:3, reveal to us that the early Christian view of Jesus as God's Son received new dimensions in and through the appearance of resurrection faith. But how can we say with any historical justification that Jesus before this had not been regarded as God's Son in a special sense by his disciples? Throughout the entire Synoptic tradition it is striking to note how intimately Jesus speaks to God and about God. It seems to me that Joachim Jeremias is too bold when he asserts that in the Jewish milieu of Jesus' time it was unthinkable to address God as "Abba" (Father). Our source material related to the way contemporary Jewish groups addressed God in prayer is too limited to enable us to say with certainty what was *not* done. But the impression derived from the Gospel tradition of Jesus' unaffected but close intimacy with God the Father remains, expressed most clearly in his use of the prayer-address *Abba*. Thus we can recognize a continuity and development in the Son of God Christology comparable to that with the title Lord.

(3) With regard to Jesus' attitude toward the title Messiah / Christ, I find it hard to avoid the impression that the contemporary discussion often suffers from a certain anachronism in the very way in which the problem is posed. We carry on our debate as though this title was already extant with its specifically Christian significance before Jesus

appeared, and as though the point in question is this: Did Jesus want to be Messiah in this sense or not? In reality the fully formed Messiah Christology of the early church was the result of a development which gave the title a rather specific content. Before Jesus came the term *Messiah* simply did not have the meaning we attach to it.

From the historical point of view the question should be whether Jesus wanted to be Messiah in the sense in which the term was commonly used among the Jews at the beginning of our era: whether he desired to be the liberator who would deliver the people of Israel from their enemies and oppressors, and secure for them political freedom (even hegemony) in addition to all spiritual blessings? It seems clear that Jesus rejected the title understood in that sense. It is another question how Jesus thought of himself and his mission, with its peculiar relation with the coming reign of God, and whether he permitted his disciples to use the Messiah title as a designation of him in this mission. These are more difficult questions, but they are of interest: in the Gospel tradition we see how Jesus corrects his disciples' picture of his own life's course as well as theirs by teaching them the necessity of humbling oneself and sacrificing oneself in accordance with the will of God. The ideal picture of Jesus, which in the course of time takes form, is given the Messiah title, and this title becomes so important that it serves as Jesus' second name. But the fact is that the significance which the early church gave this title was in large measure modeled on the picture it had of *Jesus* and no other: *his* person, *his* teaching, *his* work, *his* destiny, all interpreted in the light of the Holy Scriptures. And it is most difficult to assume that this peculiar process of development first began after Easter. For my own part, I believe that the early Christian proclamation of Jesus as Messiah had deep factual roots in Jesus' own proclamation and in his own view of himself.

We have now reviewed the three major titles used in the early Christian interpretation of Christ. In every case I find it hard to discover an original core which is of a clearly different kind than the motif we see in the mature Christology. What we do see here is a lively and changing process of development, but a development which is to a high degree *interpretative* in nature. We do not get the impression that early Christianity produced any bold innovations and projected these backward in time. It rather seems that the early church interpreted creatively something given in the tradition concerning the Lord Jesus.

A few words should perhaps be added about the genesis of the *Son of Man* Christology. This question, as is well known, is extremely complicated and controversial. The opinions of modern scholars are so diverse that one does not dare to hope for a consensus until some new manuscript has been discovered. I find it especially worth considering that early Christianity had so much difficulty in dealing with the Son of Man title. In Greek-speaking areas it could hardly be used at all. It evidently was felt to be as clumsy and hard to understand as it was misleading. Nevertheless we find this awkward term in the sayings of Jesus in the Gospels—and nearly exclusively there. This can scarcely be explained otherwise than that the early Christians felt obligated to preserve a peculiarity in Jesus' own manner of speaking. The fact that this term in the course of time appeared ever more frequently in sayings of Jesus among the evangelists also indicates that it was considered to be *typical* for the speech of Jesus. Here we have another token of conservatism and continuity in the Jesus tradition: even awkward expressions were preserved (though of course this was not always possible). We recognize again a parallel with rabbinical tradition. At the same time we can see from the content of the Son of Man texts that an interpretative development has taken place.

The question regarding continuity in the early Christian view of Jesus has a number of aspects, and one of them has, in my opinion, not received enough attention in the debate of the last generation about the history of the Gospel tradition, or in the debate concerning the christological development in early Christianity. I am thinking of the *ethical* dimension in the early church's interpretation of Jesus. Much has been written during the last generation about the relationship between Jesus and the Old Testament prophecies, but remarkably little about the relationship between Jesus and the *Law,* the basic demands of Torah. I have sought to clarify this question in a series of studies during the past decade. I have been struck by the fact that an impressive number of the sayings of Jesus in the Gospels seem to have some relation to the summarizing commandment in the Torah: "Hear, O Israel: The Lord our God is one Lord; and you shall love the Lord your God with all your heart, and with all your soul, and with all your might" (Deut. 6:4–5). It does seem obvious that Israel's confession text (*Shema‘*)—in which the command to love God is included—played a fundamental role for Jesus. And in the early Christian teaching about Jesus as the fulfiller of Torah this element has been well preserved. In this ethical dimension too there is an obvious unity, constancy, and continuity in the Jesus tradition. Unfortunately time does not permit us to examine this complicated problem more closely.*

*See the literature listed at the close of this book.

11

Personal Continuity in Early Christianity

For the pioneer form critics, Dibelius and Bultmann, it was a fundamental idea—taken over from contemporary folk-lore—that the Synoptic tradition had anonymous origins in the early Christian congregations, that it arose among people whose names are unknown. Dibelius compares the emergence and the history of this tradition to a biological process, and quotes the phrase "a biology of the saga" (*eine Biologie der Sage*). Bultmann agrees. Numerous scholars have opposed this point. Vincent Taylor points out rather drily in his book *The Formation of the Gospel Tradition:* "If the form critics are right, Jesus' disciples must have been translated to heaven immediately after the resurrection."* I would like to make some observations here about authorities and continuity of persons in early Christianity.

It is obvious that certain well-known sociopsychological mechanisms also functioned in early Christianity. We can establish, for example, that the early Christian congregations are nowhere described in our sources as gray masses of un-named equals. Everywhere we see that certain persons have greater authority than others. And clearly one of the factors which gave a man authority in the early church was what he knew about Jesus.

*(London: Macmillan & Co., 1933), p. 41.

In the New Testament Jesus is the authority with a capital *A*; he has no equal. But after his departure we find that Jesus' closest disciples are granted a position of honor specifically because they have been with Jesus (cf. Acts 1:21f.). And it is of exceptional importance in this context that their relationship to Jesus is not depicted as a vague contact but as a direct disciple relationship. The disciples have not simply seen and heard Jesus; they have received teaching from him directly. Thus we see that the first link in the chain of tradition—the one between Jesus and his closest disciples—is described as a relationship characterized by instruction given and received.

That Jesus devoted himself to *teaching* is an original and everywhere confirmed datum of the Gospel tradition in its entirety. If we survey the Gospels, and for the sake of simplicity disregard the question of the different layers in the material, we see this in many ways. Jesus' followers address him as rabbi (*rabbi*), master (*didaskalos, epistatēs*), or Lord (*Kyrios*). Those closest to him are called disciples (*mathētai*). He teaches both privately and publicly. This takes place both out in the open (at the seashore, on a mountain, and so on) as well as indoors (in synagogues or private houses). He walks from town to town and teaches. The disciples "are with him" (*einai meta, einai sun*) constantly, on weekdays and Sabbath. When Jesus makes his journeys, his disciples "follow" him (*akolouthein*). They serve him in various ways. Admittedly their relationship to the Master is not specified with a verb meaning "to serve," but we see from circumstantial reports that they do assist Jesus in different ways and carry out errands on his behalf. It appears that the group closest to Jesus lives together in a certain house in Capernaum and even stays together when on their journeys. According to John (12:6; 13:29) they also share a common purse. When Mark reports (in 3:14) about the choosing of "the Twelve," he tells us that Jesus "appointed twelve" that they might "be with him" (*hina ōsin met' autou*) and that he might send them out. From the way this is formulated it appears that the evangelist intends to say that the Twelve constituted an inner group which Jesus, during his earthly ministry, had limited and made his own spiritual family, his "house." We may compare the tradition which holds that Jesus designated his disciples as his true family (Mark 3:31–35, with par.).

As is well known, there is a lively discussion today whether the *collegium* of "the Twelve" actually existed in Jesus' time, or whether Mark simply retrojects this early Christian *collegium* back into the life of Jesus. I find it very hard to believe that the group of "the Twelve" is secondary in the Gospel tradition. One reason for this is the very role which these men play in the Gospels, for we quite clearly do not encounter here the mature, authoritative pillar figures who were looked up to in the early church. Here we meet twelve insignificant, immature disciples, lacking understanding and wisdom. If Mark had projected "the Twelve" backward to the time of Jesus, he must have been such a clever writer of history that he could at the same time bring these venerable spiritual leaders back to a strikingly youthful and immature stage. The basic hypothesis must be supported by a series of fabricated complementary hypotheses. The simplest solution, and therefore the one historically most probable, is that "the Twelve" actually were with Jesus during his earthly ministry.

If so, Jesus did not simply have a number of disciples. He had selected a group of twelve of them, given them a special position, and thereby a special authorization. This would provide a natural explanation of the great authority "the Twelve" exercised after Easter. I believe that such was the case. But I shall not proceed to argue on the basis of this judgment. Neither shall I get involved in the troublesome question regarding the early Christian *apostolate* and its connection with Jesus' authorization of "the Twelve."* I content myself with pointing to the important continuity which had its basis in the fact that Jesus had *disciples,* who subsequently were able to function as experts who knew what the Master had said and done.

The man who wrote the Gospel of Luke and the book of Acts (I call him Luke) asserts in his famous prologue that the Jesus traditions which he has put together in his work go back to those "who from the beginning were eyewitnesses and ministers of the word." He thus characterizes the Jesus material as tradition (the verb used is *paradidonai*), and he indicates those who first bore the tradition. When he refers to those "who from the beginning were eyewitnesses and ministers of the word" (*autoptai kai hypēretai tou logou*), Luke is thinking of "the Twelve." They form the nucleus of those who were present "during all the time that the Lord Jesus went in and out among us" (Acts 1:21), and subsequently devoted themselves to "the ministry of the word" (*diakonia tou logou,* 6:4). They preach and teach and heal "in Jesus' name" (Acts 3:6; 4:10, 18; 5:28, 40, etc.). They appear as Jesus' "witnesses," witnesses above all to his resurrection. It is the "apostles' teaching" (*hē didachē tōn apostolōn,* Acts 2:42) which holds the congregation together, and the early Christian congregation in Jerusalem—the mother congregation itself—grows around the nucleus composed of "the Twelve" and Jesus' mother and brothers.

It is quite clear that Luke provides us with a simplified and

---

*See my "Die Boten Gottes und die Apostel Christi," *Svensk Exegetisk Årsbok* 27 (1962): 89–131.

even tendentious picture; the beginnings of the early church were certainly a much more complicated process than Luke makes them out to be. But it is hard to deny that in certain basic respects he has the historical probabilities in his favor. Who would have taken up Jesus' fallen mantle after Easter if not his closest disciples? Who would have had greater respect as experts and witnesses than they? To whom would people go if they wanted to know what Jesus had said and done, and what really had happened when he was executed, *interpreted from within,* in the light of his own teaching?

At this point it is illuminating to take note of the simple mechanisms which functioned among the rabbis. If a person wanted to know what a given teacher, no longer living, actually taught, he would go to the teacher's disciples, to those who had heard him teach. Some people journeyed long in order to find out what a certain rabbi had taught on a given point. According to the rabbinical tradition, for example, the young Hillel is said to have traveled all the way from Babylon to Jerusalem in order to obtain information on a few issues.

It was not rank which made one a bearer of tradition. Sometimes it is asserted in the literature that only ordained rabbis could transmit the traditions. That is a purely arbitrary claim. Ordination did convey authority. But anyone who had heard and seen a teacher could (provided he was a responsible person with a tongue in his mouth) transmit what he knew. The rabbis often employed rather simple and insignificant assistants in this role. The prime requirement was that such persons had a dependable memory. In the old tract *Edujot* we can see, for example, how old practice is ascertained by seeking out knowledgeable witnesses. The status of such persons is immaterial; their knowledge of the point at issue is all that matters. In one case a question was resolved on the basis of testimony provided by two weavers—simple artisans, in other words—who had heard what Schemaiah and Abtalion had said about a certain question (Eduj. 1:3).

My contention is thus that we have every reason to proceed on the assumption that Jesus' closest disciples had an authoritative position in early Christianity as witnesses and bearers of the traditions of what Jesus had said and done. There is no reason to suppose that any believer in the early church could create traditions about Jesus and expect that his word would be accepted.

If we consider Paul, who was not himself one of Jesus' disciples during his earthly ministry and who therefore might seem an unlikely source of support for the points of view presented here, we find, contrary to expectation, significant information which leads in the same direction. Even though he had to struggle energetically to assert his own freedom and sovereignty as an apostle, he nevertheless discloses something of the authoritative status of the mother congregation and its men of repute (*hoi dokountes*)—men such as Peter, James, and John and the group in Jerusalem to whom Peter refers as "those who were apostles before me" (*hoi pro emou apostoloi,* Gal. 1:17).

In 1 Corinthians Paul describes himself as a bearer of tradition. He has delivered to the congregations Jesus traditions which he himself has received. He stands therefore in a chain of tradition. In 1 Cor. 4:14–17 we find (as noted above) a most interesting statement. Paul here admonishes the congregation in Corinth to imitate him as he imitates Christ; and, in order to assist the congregation in this regard, he sends to them his beloved and faithful son Timothy to remind them of his "ways," that is, the doctrines and practices he proclaims in all of his congregations. Thus we have here an example of tradition proceeding from an apostle to a congregation via the apostle's disciple. As we know, the postapostolic literature provides us with more examples of such chains of personal continuity in the early church; this occurred even though the gospel was being spread in book form as well by that time.

It is also important to remember the personal continuity which the evangelists themselves represent. The Gospels are not collections of tradition hundreds of years old. The Gospel of Mark was written no more than forty years after Jesus was crucified, the other three no more than thirty years after Mark. Mark at least wrote while many eyewitnesses were still living, and he evidently was personally acquainted with all of the leading members of the Jesus circle in Jerusalem, as well as with Paul. The author of the Lukan writings is also probably a man named in the New Testament—the Luke who was Paul's co-worker. Those behind the Gospels of Matthew and John are more difficult to identify. But in these cases too we have reason to believe that they had been in personal contact with eyewitnesses.

These perspectives have not been given due weight in the Gospel research of the form-critical era. It seems as though parallels from folklore—that is, material extending over centuries of time and wide areas of space—have tempted scholars unconsciously to stretch out the chronological and geographical dimensions of the formation of the early Christian tradition in an unreasonable manner. What is needed here is a more sober approach to history. In the New Testament period the church was not nearly as widespread or as large in numbers as we usually imagine.

12

From Jesus to the Gospels

I have previously touched upon one of the most perplexing aspects of the documents preserved from early Christianity: the isolation of the Jesus tradition. In the New Testament we have on the one hand the three synoptic Gospels with traditions from and about Jesus. In them we find direct quotations of words Jesus is said to have spoken during his earthly ministry, and direct reports of what he is said to have done while at work in Israel. The mystery of Jesus is not presented here in the framework of proclamation, teaching, or admonition. We find here that a number of independent words and narratives have been brought together to form an acount of a bygone period in the history of salvation. The fact that there is an *edifying intention* in the evangelists' presentation in no way belies this assertion.

On the other hand, we find in the New Testament a number of letters written by early Christian authorities to Christian congregations in the period of the early church. They bear the names of Paul, Peter, John, James, and Jude. These letters give us a reasonable idea of how men preached and taught and admonished in the first Christian congregations. In these letters we find practically no direct quotations of what Jesus had said or reports of what he had done during his earthly ministry. The authors seem to presuppose such material, to allude to it, to build further upon its content, to instruct in the same spirit, and so on, but they virtually never quote.

This simple state of affairs makes it immensely difficult for me to accept the assertion of many form critics that the Synoptic tradition has arisen and been preserved in the general preaching and teaching and exhortation of the early Christian congregations. Questions as to from where the evangelists took this *isolated* Jesus tradition and how it was handed on in the early church before the Gospels were written have not received acceptable answers from the form critics.

I have already pointed out that in 1 Corinthians (chaps. 11 and 15) Paul seems to provide us with a clue that guides us to the answer to these questions. It seems from what Paul says in these two chapters that regular acts of transmitting texts occurred in early Christianity; that is, when the need arose, one or more Jesus traditions were handed on to a recipient, either in written form or by impressing the text upon the memory. If in written form, it must have involved unofficial notes: "secret scrolls" as the rabbis called them, or "memoranda" as the Greek teachers referred to them, but not complete books. It is most likely, however, that Paul is referring to oral transmission in these passages.

Now we shall pose this question: Can we perceive in the *Gospels* anything which would indicate that textual transmission of this kind was already taking place while Jesus was active in Galilee and Jerusalem?

If one examines the words of Jesus in the synoptic Gospels —sayings and parables—one is struck by their artistic form. The English scholar C. F. Burney wrote a captivating book on this topic over fifty years ago now (*The Poetry of Our*

*Lord).** More recent authors have supplemented Burney's observations, among others, Joachim Jeremias.†

The sayings of Jesus in the synoptic Gospels do not have the character of everyday words or of casual repartee. Nor can they be arbitrarily selected portions of sermons or of doctrinal discourses. Rather they consist of brief, laconic, well-rounded texts, of pointed statements with a clear profile, rich in content and poetic in form. The artistic devices show through clearly even in the tradition's Greek form: picturesque content, strophic construction, *parallelismus membrorum,* verbatim repetition, and so on. This can be seen all the more clearly if one translates these texts back into Aramaic. Then one sees in the sayings of Jesus such characteristics as rhythm, assonance, and alliteration as well. It is obvious that we are dealing here with carefully thought out and deliberately formulated statements.

We can also see in the Gospels that early Christianity had a summary designation for texts of this kind. In Greek they were called *parabolai* (pl.). The term is used not only in reference to narrative parables of various kinds (e.g., Matt. 13), but also in reference to brief word pictures and sayings (e.g., the saying "there is nothing outside a man which by going into him can defile him," Mark 7:15, 17; cf. 4:33 and Luke 4:23.) It was typical of Jesus' way of teaching to do so with the aid of *parabolai.*

Behind the Greek *parabolē* (sing.) are the Hebrew *māshāl* (pl. *meschālim* or *meschālot*) and the Aramaic *matlā.* These words were used for picturesque sayings, whether they were

---

The Poetry of Our Lord: An Examination of the Formal Elements of Hebrew Poetry in the Discourses of Jesus Christ (Oxford: Oxford University Press, 1925).
†See, e.g., *Neutestamentliche Theologie* (Gütersloh: Gütersloher Verlagshaus, 1971), Part 1, pp. 124-38. English Translation: *New Testament Theology* (New York: Charles Scribner's Sons, 1971), pp. 14-29.

short or long, as distinct from more ordinary, everyday speech: a metaphor, a parable, an allegory, a fable, a maxim, a riddle, a folk song, or whatever. As we know, the proverbs in the Book of Proverbs are called *meshālim*; the book's Hebrew name is *Mishle Shelomo,* "Solomon's meshalim." In the Old Testament we also find an old designation for the men who were known for their ability to transmit traditional words of wisdom and to formulate sayings of their own. They were called *moshelim,* that is, tellers of parables, makers of proverbs, men of pithy speech.

What we see here is how Jesus' teaching can be judged from a *purely formal* point of view. He did not teach in such a way that he can be classified as a teacher of the law (a *halakist*). One might classify him as a *haggadist,* inasmuch as the term *haggādā* was sufficiently vague to be applicable to all nonjuridical teaching. But that classification is not very helpful; one can be more precise. According to the express testimony of the early Christian sources, Jesus taught with the aid of *meshālim,* in Greek *parabolai,* that is, parables and sayings. He was—if we may employ an ancient designation—a *moshel,* a parabolist, one who spoke in parables and pithy sayings.

This does not mean that he was purely and simply a popular wisdom teacher of the old type. From the content of his teaching we see that he at times could utilize traditional wisdom, but for the most part he spoke in his own original way about the reign of God, both of its external, obvious characteristics, as well as of its inner secrets, its "mysteries." He had a message—the kerygma concerning the reign of God—and he presented it with the aid of parables and sayings (as well as deeds). We also note that this was done in a prophetic spirit, and with messianic authority. Jesus appears in the synoptic Gospels as a personage who combines a variety of traits from the ancient heritage of Israel's different men of God. And he is not simply one teacher among many. He breaks through the usual categories. It is typical that he is described as "more than" Solomon, "more than" Jonah, David's "Lord," and so on. When I describe him as a *moshel* (a parabolist) I do so simply to characterize from a purely *formal* point of view the way in which he shaped his oral teaching.

If we analyze this kind of saying, we note that the wording itself is of great importance. The intent here is not simply to instruct or to clarify in general terms, but to provide the listeners with certain "words" to ponder and discuss. The speaker in this context does not engage his hearers in conversation, nor does he lecture them, but rather presents them with a parable; he delivers a proverb to them. They receive it somewhat in the way one receives a curious object which one must examine in order to find out how it can be used. They are given a text upon which they can ruminate and discuss with one another in an effort to clarify its meaning. What is most important here is, of course, not that people learn the text, but that they understand its meaning—but much of the meaning is dependent on the wording.

If one looks at the *form* which these sayings take, one notes that they are brief, pointed, and pregnant. The sayings have been formulated so that they can be easily remembered. As we know, the Gospels tell us that Jesus "spoke in *meshālim*" (parables), "taught in *meshālim*" or "set forth a *māshāl*" for his listeners. Such statements can scarcely mean that Jesus presented the text in question one time only, expecting that those who heard it would remember it and be able to understand it. In the light of the ancient Jewish methods of teaching, it seems entirely clear to me that Jesus presented such a saying two or more times in an effort to impress it upon the minds ("hearts") of his hearers. Among the rabbis we can see—though the oldest evidence dates from after the fall of the Temple—how evident it was that a teacher would repeat the texts until his pupils knew them by heart; four repetitions seem to have been common.

The evangelists maintain that Jesus regularly presented *meshālim* in his public teaching and when necessary *interpreted* these for his disciples. This applies both to *meshālim* of the type we call parables (Mark 4, Matt. 13, Luke 8) and to those we call logia (Mark 7, Matt. 15). The evangelists thus describe not only occasions on which Jesus presents such texts, but also situations in which he comments upon them; note for example such terms as *epilyein* (explain, interpret) in Mark 4:34; *diasafein* (explain, expound) in Matt. 13:36; *frazein* (interpret) in Matt. 15:15. One cannot exclude the possibility that the scenes described in the parable chapter and in the chapter dealing with clean and unclean eating were drawn up for the first time at a later stage. But there are scarcely tenable grounds for the suspicion that the teaching pattern as such lacks historical foundation.* Here we cannot be dealing with a simple backdating of teaching scenes from the time of the early church. And there is no reason to believe that texts of this kind were of interest only after Easter. If Jesus created *meshālim* during his public ministry, it is reasonable to assume that his disciples preserved these texts right from the beginning. They must have fixed them in their memories, pondered them, and discussed them. Otherwise they were not his disciples. Why would the disciples not have been interested in these texts *prior to Easter*?

In an essay by Heinz Schürmann which I mentioned a bit earlier (*Die vorösterlichen Anfänge der Logientradition*), the

---

*See David Daube, *The New Testament and Rabbinic Judaism* (London: The Athlone Press, 1956), pp. 141–50.

author has emphasized that even from a purely form-critical point of view one must reckon with the fact that Jesus' followers began to preserve a tradition of sayings even before Easter. He refers among other things to the fact that according to the Gospels Jesus, during his ministry in Galilee, sent out his disciples to preach and to heal. This "sending" has such a strong anchoring in the tradition that, all things being considered, it cannot be dismissed as a simple backdating of the early Christian missionary activity after Easter (Mark 6:7-13, with par., Luke 10:1-16). Schürmann then points out that Jesus must have given these immature and unlearned disciples certain instructions about what they were to preach before he sent them out. Here then is a situation in which we must assume that Jesus imprinted his teaching in the minds of his disciples.

To this I would add that all teaching in *meshālim* must reasonably be of this kind. If Jesus taught in parables and logia, in all probability he taught his hearers these texts. My contention is that the very form of the sayings of Jesus indicates that they were never *integrated* parts of an expansive, continuous presentation. And I maintain for that reason that nothing suggests that these words were of interest only after Easter. On the contrary, everything suggests that devoted disciples had memorized them when their Master taught them during his ministry in Galilee and Jerusalem.

Here then we have a point of departure. Jesus presented *meshālim* for his hearers, and the disciples were the first to memorize them, to ponder them, and to discuss together what they meant. In the beginning was Jesus' kerygma concerning the reign of God. The oldest components in the Gospel tradition are certainly in principle the parables and the logia which served to make this kerygma concrete.

In view of the fact that the disciples had begun to preserve

Jesus' teachings in this way, it was quite natural that narrative texts about Jesus also appeared in order to supplement the *meshālim*. An intermediary form between the sayings tradition and the narrative tradition consists of those elements in the tradition which Dibelius calls "paradigms" and Bultmann "apophthegms." These are sayings of Jesus which are provided with a brief narrative introduction. The sayings themselves are certainly the most important here, but one must put them in context, briefly indicating the situation in which they were uttered, in order to make them comprehensible. It is easy to imagine how such expanded "sayings traditions" were added to the memorized material. And from the apophthegms it is not far to those elements in the tradition which sum up a conversation.

As far as the narrative material proper is concerned, it is also easy to imagine how certain elements soon came into the picture. I am thinking of reports of certain things that Jesus had done and which were understood to be symbolic actions. Here the *māshāl* lay in the deed itself, but if one wanted to prompt another who had not seen what was done to think about its meaning and discuss it, then it was obviously necessary to formulate a report about the deed.

It is not possible to treat all narrative traditions in one and the same way. The detailed accounts which Dibelius refers to as "tales" (*Novellen*) provide particular problems in this context. Nonetheless, I think that one can easily imagine how the narrative traditions quite naturally came to supplement the sayings traditions. Jesus had not presented himself in word alone. He had also done a number of characteristic deeds. He was known as one who could miraculously heal the sick and expel demons. It would have been unnatural to preserve only the sayings of such a man.

With regard to the Passion story, the groundwork of the narrative was certainly laid soon after Easter, for early Christianity had here received its most puzzling *māshāl*: Why was it necessary for Jesus to "suffer these things and enter into his glory" (cf. Luke 24:26)?

The clarity to which the early church came with regard to the meaning of the suffering, death, and resurrection of Jesus was accompanied by a clarity as to his identity and peculiar status as Messiah. Now a complete picture of Jesus had emerged and it was possible to interpret the individual traditions in the light of a strong, unified conviction about who Jesus actually was, and to organize the tradition material on the basis of all-encompassing principles. It would be hard to prove that this insight was first gained in the Hellenistic branch of Christianity. I also find it difficult to prove that the church's understanding of the mystery of Jesus after Easter was a fundamentally *different* picture from the provisional one which Jesus had sought to give to his disciples during his days on earth (even though many misunderstandings obviously remained at the time of the crucifixion). In principle it seems to be only a clearer and more complete picture. The same holds true of the relationship between Jesus' kerygma of the reign of God and the church's post-Easter kerygma. The church's kerygma about Christ was by all the evidence little other than a more concrete, precise, and fully developed version of Jesus' message about the reign of God. The enigmatic could now—at least in part—be proclaimed clearly.

When we speak of the *connection* between the individual elements in the tradition, it is important that we do not limit our perspective to the form-historical thesis that the separate elements arose completely independently of one another and stood from the beginning entirely on their own without any inner, organic relationship. That does not seem to have been the case. A number of scholars, including C. H. Dodd, H. Riesenfeld, and H. Simonsen, have demonstrated that many of the tradition elements in the Gospels quite simply presuppose others or point ahead to others. Furthermore, one sees time after time that the early Christian traditionist knew more about Jesus than he could have derived directly from the wording of the tradition elements. Relevant here are the many observations which point to the fact that early Christianity already had, in its earliest phase of development, a general picture of Jesus and a rough outline of his life's fate, with emphasis on his death and resurrection. New audiences had to be provided with this orientation.

These observations deserve our careful attention if we wish to have a balanced understanding of the origin and history of the Synoptic tradition. It will not do to *limit* one's perspective to the idea that the individual elements in the tradition are prior to the redactional patterns used in gathering the materials. The history of the origins of the Synoptic tradition is not only the history of how the various parts arose and were assembled, but also the history of *the interaction between the whole and the parts,* between the total view and the concrete formation of the material, which certainly took place during the entire tradition formation process.

A further problem of relevance here concerns the transition from oral tradition to writings. This was certainly a drawn-out and involved process. As I have already suggested, private notes were probably made rather early. As time went on, blocks of tradition, large and small, have been put together, and eventually the time was ripe for the first Gospel in our sense of the word. This whole area is full of difficult questions. For example, what happens when oral tradition of just *this* kind is put into writing; how in such cases does tradition subsequently influence what is written; and what is written, tradition? The influence here is obviously reciprocal, but I cannot pursue this further at this time.

I do not believe that there is any *simple* answer to the question concerning the origins of the Gospel tradition. There is certainly a complicated development behind our synoptic Gospels—to say nothing about the Gospel of John, which, as far as I can see, has its own history. But I believe that there is historical justification, based on sound historical judgments, for concluding that there is an unbroken path which leads from Jesus' teaching in *meshālim* to the early church's methodical handing on of Jesus texts, a transmission carried on for *its own sake*. In other words, this was done not only in order that the recipients might come to faith or be strengthened in their love, but also for the specific reason that they should *have* these indispensable texts. I am referring to those activities in early Christianity by which Jesus texts were transmitted, either orally or in written form. Paul discloses in 1 Corinthians 11 and 15 that such took place. History does not follow only theological lines. As an historian, one must pay attention to trivial and practical circumstances as well. The early Christian congregations did not live only on preaching and theology. They had practical things to see about too, such as procuring sacred Scriptures. They had also, I contend, quite practically to secure Jesus tradition for themselves, and this in spite of the fact that faith comes neither by copying texts nor by learning to recite them.

13

"The Whole Truth"

In what has been written to this point I have attempted in a brief, outline manner to indicate why I believe that the Gospels essentially provide us with an historically reliable picture of Jesus of Nazareth. This applies primarily to the synoptic Gospels. Among other reasons, the four following arguments speak in favor of the view that the continuity and reliability of the early Christian tradition have been preserved without interruption:

(1) The early Christian congregations were not shapeless communities in which spiritual goods were created anonymously. All the sources from early Christianity indicate that already in its first stages certain leaders and teachers occupied positions of authority in the congregations and that these men were in contact with one another. "The Twelve," with Peter at their head, had a central authority which even Paul had to take into account. We can see chains of tradition delineated in the material: Peter was Jesus' disciple, Paul knew Peter (Gal. 1:18; 2:1-14), Timothy was Paul's disciple (1 Cor. 4:16f.), and so on.

(2) In the synoptic Gospels, no later "high Christology" has been able to efface the characteristic picture of an earthly Jesus. Typical features of his appearance in Israel have been preserved: he appears with power (*exousia*) as a mysterious

but authoritative representative of the coming reign of God; he proclaims that reign (in the form of *meshālim*); he expounds God's demands on those who are to enter the reign of God; he heals the sick, expels demons, and sets this activity in relation to the reign of God; he is generous to the religious and social outcasts in Israel to the point of giving offence, which is not the least of the reasons why he comes in conflict with the leaders of his people; he dies for his cause and that of the reign of God, and so on. This is no simple backdating of the faith in Christ manifested in the church after Easter.

(3) One feature which sharply distinguishes the formation of the early Christian tradition from the formation of popular traditions in general is that the former takes place in continuous contact with authoritative sacred Scriptures. Jesus himself taught in association with the Holy Scriptures, and the Synoptic material clearly had this same association the whole time until it was finally written down. This association had an enriching but obviously also a stabilizing effect on the tradition.*

(4) Even with regard to the wording of the Jesus tradition —and here primarily that of the sayings tradition—the Gospels reflect the fact that the material has been preserved with respect and care.

The sources give us no reason to believe that just anyone in the early Christian period could say that Jesus had said anything whatever. I maintain that Jesus' closest disciples—Peter, James, John and the group known as "the Twelve"—must be suspected of having had much to do with the oldest stages of the Synoptic tradition. They preserved Jesus' *meshālim—*

---

*See Ellis, "Form Criticism," pp. 299-315.

parables, logia—and began to tell of his activities even while he was conducting his own ministry before Easter.

It is difficult to answer the question to what extent the Synoptic material was assembled in various collections by "the Twelve" during their activity in Jerusalem in the first phase of the mother congregation there. Luke's presentation in his Gospel (1:1–4) and in the Book of Acts has an a priori probability at its center: who would have continued the Master's work if not the members of his innermost circle of disciples? But Luke obviously provides a highly simplified, tendentious, and stylized picture of a complicated historical process. There certainly were persons "working with the word" in congregations other than the one in Jerusalem; they too preserved the words of Jesus and narratives about him, discussed and interpreted them, and all of this in connection with an intensive "examination" of the Holy Scriptures (cf. Acts 17:11). None of the evangelists worked with traditions taken only from one source.

It thus seems historically very probable that the Jesus traditions in the Gospels have been preserved for us by men both reliable and well informed. But even the one who has come to this point of view sees directly in our Gospels that the Jesus traditions must have undergone certain changes on the way from Jesus to the different evangelists. If one places the three Synoptic versions side by side—that is, by looking in a synopsis—one can see immediately how they differ from one another. It is thus uncontestable that changes took place in this material in the process of its transmission (as well as in that of its final redaction). The only question is how extensive these changes can have been. We shall now in conclusion touch briefly upon this question.

There were a number of factors which brought about the changes in this material, but it is not necessary to list them all. One important factor to keep in mind is the *transfer of the material* from Aramaic and Hebrew *to Greek*. Admittedly this occurred in a multilingual milieu, where the traditions were found side by side in the original language and in Greek and where so many people knew both languages that the translations could for a long time be checked and corrected. Nonetheless it is well known that no translation can be completely identical with the original and that two or more translations will never be word for word the same. The prologue to the Book of Sirach indicates that these observations are not new.

Particularly significant changes can hardly have taken place with the translation into Greek, however. Greater significance must be attached to the changes which occurred during the ongoing *interpretation* of the traditions, in the efforts to understand Jesus' words and deeds more fully and comprehensively and to discover their importance for the problems and questions which confronted the congregations in their day. There are clear signs of this activity in the Gospels, indications of what we can call early Christianity's *work with the word*.

In each of the Gospels we see reflected the early church's consciousness of the fact that Jesus' closest followers did not understand him particularly well during his earthly ministry and that many aspects of the truth did not dawn upon them until after Easter. A couple of quotations from the Gospel of John put it in a nutshell. In John 12:12–16 the evangelist reports on Jesus' entry into Jerusalem. He makes this comment: "His disciples did not understand this at first, but when Jesus was glorified, then they remembered that this had been written of him and had been done to him." In 2:19–22 Jesus, in the course of his teaching in Jerusalem, pronounces the logion concerning the destruction of the Temple and its rebuilding in three days. Afterward John comments: "When therefore he was raised from the dead, his disciples remembered that he had said this; and they believed the scripture and the word which Jesus had spoken." Here we see how conscious the evangelist is of the fact that certain of Jesus' words and deeds were not clear to the disciples until after the resurrection. We note further that the explanation of Jesus' words and of what happened to him is connected with the interpretation of the sacred Scriptures.

John (I call the man behind the Fourth Gospel by this name without going into the question who he really was) gives us his own explanation of the fact that the church understands Jesus more fully after Easter. In his farewell address, the Johannine Jesus says: "But the Counselor, the Holy Spirit, whom the Father will send in my name, he will teach you all things, and bring to your remembrance all that I have said to you" (14:26). And later on, in this same farewell speech, Jesus says: "When the Spirit of truth comes, he will guide you into all the truth . . . He will glorify me, for he will take what is mine and declare it to you" (16:13f.).

These passages (and several similar ones) in the Gospel of John provide us with insights into the way in which the post-Easter situation is seen from within the Johannine circle. We see here the deliberateness with which they work with the Jesus tradition, striving better to understand both it and the sacred Scriptures. They feel that the Lord himself has authorized them to do this, the Lord who has been glorified and who has sent his Spirit to guide the church into "the whole truth." In this situation, and with this certainty, they feel free to develop—to embellish—the content of the Jesus tradition. After all, it is the Spirit who leads the church into "the whole truth"! In the Johannine congregations the margin for the free rendering of the significance of Jesus' words appears to have been remarkably large. The Johannine Jesus seems to be speaking through the mouth of his early Christian interpreters. To put it in rabbinical terms, one could say that the early Christian interpreters (*meturgemānim*) here stand between us and the laconic, earthly Jesus.

Nevertheless, there is in the Gospel of John an express desire to stand firmly on historical ground. When the evangelist at the original conclusion of the Gospel (20:30–31)—chapter 21 is, as we know, an appendix—writes about the purpose of the book, he says: "Now Jesus did many other signs in the presence of the disciples, which are not written in this book; but these are written that you may believe that Jesus is the Christ, the Son of God, and that believing, you may have life in his name." The evangelist writes with a clear tendentiousness: the faith of his readers is to be preserved and strengthened. But he intends to present that which Jesus did "in the presence of the disciples." The degree to which the evangelist's presentation of the tradition material has been governed by his edifying tendentiousness can be seen very clearly in the individual pericopes in the Fourth Gospel.

It is well known that the differences between the Gospel of John and the synoptic Gospels are significant. John seems in certain essential respects to have built upon a different branch of the tradition than the synoptics, and to have treated the tradition material much more freely than the men behind the Synoptics felt free to do. At the same time, however, the clues given in John's Gospel seem to be of help as we seek to clarify the history of the Synoptic tradition as well.

It is entirely clear that the elements of the Synoptic tradition have been open to changes of *one* kind: those made in an effort to clarify the *meaning* of the transmitted texts, to clarify "the whole truth" for the Christian congregations. I usually label changes of this kind *interpretative adaptations.* Even where the sayings of Jesus are concerned, it seems that liberty to make minor alterations in the wording in an effort to bring out the meaning was permitted (note, e.g., the various predictions of suffering). Nothing has hindered the creation in this way of several variants of one and the same Jesus saying, which have then been preserved in the event that all or some of the meanings were thought worth keeping. We often see, however, that the various interpretations of one and the same Jesus saying have been brought out primarily by the evangelist by placing the saying in a certain context or by reformulating the notices in the framework and the narrative material in the Gospels. These portions of the material have been reshaped with significantly greater liberty than the wording of the sayings of Jesus themselves.

Is not the observation that the Jesus traditions have undergone alterations all the evidence one needs to refute the thesis that early Christianity has handed down the Gospel material as memorized texts? Many think so, but I have never understood this objection. We can see even in the rabbinical tradition that the material was altered in the course of time. Even in the collections of legal regulations, which are usually passed on with such extreme regard for the precise wording, changes do occur. Additions and subtractions were made.* Careful transmission thus does not prevent teachers with authority from making editorial alterations in texts and col-

*See my *Memory and Manuscript,* pp. 77–78, 97–98, 111, 136–39, 146–48, 180–81, 334–35.

lections of texts. And if we proceed from *halakic* collections of traditions to other types of texts—those with midrashic and haggadic materials (logia, parables, etc.)—we note that the wording can vary even more. Careful oral transmission— with texts learned by heart—thus does not exclude alterations in texts. What often happens here is an interaction between transmission and editorial alteration.

If one compares the different versions of one and the same tradition in the synoptic Gospels, one notes that the variations are not often so general as to give us reason to speak of a fluid tradition which gradually became fixed. The alterations are not of such a nature as they would have been had originally elastic material been formulated in different ways. The tradition elements seem to have possessed a remarkably fixed wording. Variations generally take the form of additions, omissions, transpositions, or alterations of single details in a wording which otherwise is left unchanged. (I here ignore instances in which the evangelist has restructured an entire text.) The English scholar T. W. Manson once wrote with his usual pertinence that the early church "remembered better than it understood." The preservation of the wording of the texts and the interpretation of their meaning seem not always to have kept the same pace. This is an observation which is easily explained if the material transmitted is in the form of fixed texts handed down either in written or oral—memorized—form, or, of course, in both of these forms.

The apostles and teachers of early Christianity have thus stood in the situation where they were to preach about a Lord alive in the present but also proclaim that a significant part of this Lord's saving activity had been carried out in the past (albeit rather recently), and that here on earth, in Israel. It was important both that they present a true picture of this work and that they give it an adequate interpretation for the present. Early Christianity had reason both to preserve the Jesus tradition faithfully and to interpret it with insight. The incentive for both was present.

How large a margin for reformulation and renewal of the text traditions did the men behind the Synoptic tradition have? How much freedom did they feel to transform, and to introduce explanatory elements into the Jesus tradition? I believe that this margin was in general rather limited, but there are tradition elements which indicate that at times remarkably large liberties could be taken.

I have investigated, for example, the long version of the narrative of how Jesus is tempted after being baptized, in Matt. 4:1-11 and Luke 4:1-13.* The account appears to be a tradition from Jesus' earthly activity, even though he is not yet surrounded by disciples. And it seems to contain certain undeniably historical elements: that Jesus was baptized by John the Baptist may be considered a reliable historical fact; nor is it improbable that Jesus went out into the wilderness for a time after the baptism, and that this was a time of testing for him. But otherwise the long version of the tempta-tion story must be throughout a creation of certain early Christian scribes. It is a prologue to Jesus' public ministry in Israel. For the readers of the Gospel it serves to clarify the mystery that Jesus did not intend to "seek his own good" but to accomplish the will of God in word and deed, as it is revealed in Torah. To be more precise, the account is designed to show that Jesus has heard and understood and is prepared to observe (or "to do") the summary command-

*The Testing of God's Son (Matt. 4:1-11 & Par.): An Analysis of an Early Christian Midrash (Lund: C. W. K. Gleerup, 1966).

ment in Torah (Deut. 6:4f.): "Hear, O Israel: the Lord our God is one Lord; and you shall love the Lord your God with all your heart [the first temptation], and with all your soul [the second temptation], and with all your might [the third temptation]." In a case like this the early Christian interpretation of the Jesus tradition has been remarkably free and creative in character. The tradition did provide points of contact—*there was something to interpret*—but in this instance it was interpreted with artistic freedom.

Now it is possible to explain this kind of element in the Gospel tradition. We can see in the Jewish *Targum* tradition that the men who translated the old Hebrew texts into the Aramaic of the people in the worship services could when necessary introduce interpretations into their translations. They clearly saw—or heard—what the Hebrew did and did not say. Nonetheless they could inject interpretative elements into the text, even brief stories, in an effort to clarify its meaning. In a book about the baptism of Jesus, Fritzleo Lentzen-Deis has shed some very helpful light on this matter.* It seems that the early Christian traditionists took this same type of liberty on occasion, as, for example, when they reported on the baptism and temptation of Jesus. The Matthean and Lukan versions of the temptation narrative reveal this. I am still not clear about the number of texts in the synoptic Gospels that belong in this advanced category. Presumably there are not many. The temptation story is in many respects unique. But the fact that this account is found in the synoptic Gospels tells us that early Christianity occasionally permitted itself to take great liberties—or shall we say creativity—in its effort not only to hand down the texts of

Die Taufe Jesu nach den Synoptikern (Frankfurt am Main: J. Knecht, 1970).

what Jesus had said and done, but also to interpret their mysteries for the listening congregation.

Thus there can be no doubt but that the Jesus traditions in the synoptic Gospels have undergone revisions within the early church on their way from Jesus to the evangelists. Nor can there be any doubt but that the evangelists themselves have revised their material; all who have looked into this with open eyes know this. The most interesting and significant alterations in the tradition elements and additions to the collections result, as I understand it, from the desire of the early church to *understand* the transmitted material more deeply and comprehensively and to present it as clearly as possible to those who heard the gospel. That the congregations' current needs and problems influenced this process of interpretation is in the very nature of the case; among the merits of the form critics is the fact that they have increased our awareness of this.

Insights and convictions which gradually came to the fore in the early years of Christian history have thus colored the old material derived from Jesus' ministry. To assert this does not mean, however, that one has adopted the attitude of the skeptical form critics. It is one thing to take these changes in the transmitted material in all seriousness, and quite another thing to presume that the early church freely constructed the Jesus traditions, placed the words of early Christian prophets and teachers in Jesus' mouth, and so on. One can say—with a degree of simplification—that the form critics (in any case, Bultmann and his disciples) have regarded the Synoptic tradition as a post-Easter creation of the early church. My position is that one must proceed on the belief that the Synoptic material in principle comes from the earthly Jesus and the disciples who followed him during his ministry, but that one must also do full justice to the fact that this memory material has been marked by the insights and interpretations gradually arrived at by the early Christian teachers.

I have been able, within the framework of these lectures, to do no more than *sketch* my position regarding the question of the historical credibility of the Gospels. It has not been possible to discuss the details of statements made about Jesus in the Gospels. Nevertheless, I hope that I have been able to point to reasons for the viewpoint that in the synoptic Gospels we hear not only a whisper of the voice of Jesus, but are confronted with faithfully preserved words from the mouth of Jesus and reports which in the *end* go back to those who were with Jesus during his ministry in Galilee and Jerusalem. It is true that the accounts of Jesus' life and, to a certain degree, even the sayings of Jesus have been reworked by the early church, but the primary goal in all of this has been to understand them better.

In order to prevent misunderstanding, I should perhaps add an observation of a theological nature. If our desire is to understand *the original nature of Christian faith,* it is of decisive importance for us to study carefully the development of the Jesus tradition after Easter, that is, between the time of Jesus' earthly ministry and the time when the evangelists wrote the Gospels. We must also be clear about the message—in its entirety and in its parts—of the different evangelists themselves as it is seen in its final, fixed form. In other words, we must not look upon the tradition's development and alteration as a trivial process, without importance, nor as a corruption of something that was clearest when Jesus walked about in Galilee. The evangelists tell us repeatedly that the earthly Jesus was a riddle to his people and, to a large extent, even to his disciples. Their understanding of him and his message was, before Easter, imperfect and provisional. It was not until after Easter that the disciples thought they had achieved a clear and fully correct understanding of the mystery of Jesus. It was only then that they recognized the complete meaning of the confession "You are the Christ, the Son of the living God." It was only then that they could see with full clarity Jesus' own place in the kerygma of the reign of God: his death and resurrection took a central place in the mysteries of the reign of God. This increased clarity influenced the Jesus tradition. For this reason, one of the major tasks of the New Testament theologian is the analysis of the Jesus tradition's alterations and development, the study of the process which led Jesus' disciples to "the whole truth," to use John's words. Today, presumably, we can see more clearly than at the beginning of Christian history how *diversified* this "whole truth" was within the different congregations in the early church. But we can also see unity in the midst of this diversity. If the tradition did in fact develop roughly as I have sought to sketch above, then we can maintain that the different voices in the early church's mixed choir wanted to sing a common song: the song about the incomparable One, who has been elevated by God to the heavenly realm, but only after a mysterious ministry on earth.

Bibliography

OTHER WORKS BY BIRGER GERHARDSSON

*Concerning the ancient Jewish and early Christian
methods of transmission:*

Memory and Manuscript: Oral Tradition and Written Transmission in Rabbinic Judaism and Early Christianity. 2d ed.
Uppsala and Lund: C. W. K. Gleerup, 1964. With numerous
references to sources and secondary literature.

Tradition and Transmission in Early Christianity. Lund: C. W. K.
Gleerup, 1964. Includes responses to critical reviews and
other contributions to the discussion of the main theme of the
previous book.

Concerning the early Christian apostolate:

"Die Boten Gottes und die Apostel Christi." *Svensk Exegetisk
Årsbok* 27 (1962): 89–131.

*Concerning early Christianity's "work with the word,"
particularly that related to the
confessional text Shema':*

*The Testing of God's Son (Matt. 4:1–11 & Par.): An Analysis of an
Early Christian Midrash.* Part 1. Lund: C. W. K. Gleerup,
1966.

"The Parable of the Sower and its Interpretation." *New Testament
Studies* 14 (1967/68): 165–93.

"Jésus livré et abandonné d' après la passion selon Saint Matthieu." *Revue Biblique* 76 (1969): 206–27.

"Ur Matteusevangeliet." Commentary on chaps. 1, 2, 5, 6, 7, 26, 27, 28. In *Ur Nya Testamentet,* 2d ed., edited by L. Hartman, pp. 108–50, 163–201. Lund: C. W. K. Gleerup, 1972.

"Einige Bemerkungen zu Apg. 4, 32." *Studia Theologica* 24 (1970): 142–49.

"Bibelns ethos." In *Etik och kristen tro,* 2d ed., edited by Gustaf Wingren, pp. 13–92. Lund: C. W. K. Gleerup, 1978.

"Geistiger Opferdienst nach Matth 6, 1–6, 16–21." In *Neues Testament und Geschichte. Festschrift* in honor of O. Cullmann, pp. 69–77. Zürich: Theologischer Verlag, 1972. Tübingen: J. C. B. Mohr, 1972.

"Du Judéo-christianisme à Jésus par le Shemá." In *Judéo-christianisme. Festschrift* in honor of J. Daniélou, pp. 23–36. Paris: Beauchesne, 1972.

"The Seven Parables in Matthew XIII." *New Testament Studies* 19 (1972/73): 16–37.

"Gottes Sohn als Diener Gottes." *Studia Theologica* 27 (1973): 73–106.

"The Hermeneutic Program in Matt. 22:37–40." In *Jews, Greeks and Christians. Festschrift* in honor of W. D. Davies, pp. 129–50. Leiden: E. J. Brill, 1976.

"1 Kor 13." In *Donum gentilicium. Festschrift* in honor of D. Daube, pp. 185–209. Oxford: Clarendon Press, 1978.

OTHER RELEVANT SWEDISH STUDIES (in English)

Riesenfeld, H. *The Gospel Tradition and Its Beginnings: A Study in the Limits of "Formgeschichte."* London: A. R. Mowbray, 1957. Also in *The Gospel Tradition,* pp. 1–29. Philadelphia: Fortress Press, 1970.

Stendahl, Krister. *The School of St. Matthew and Its Use of the Old Testament.* Uppsala and Lund: C. W. K. Gleerup, 1954. 2d ed. Philadelphia: Fortress Press, 1968.

Hartman, L. *Prophecy Interpreted.* Uppsala and Lund: C. W. K. Gleerup, 1966.

Olsson, B. *Structure and Meaning in the Fourth Gospel.* Uppsala and Lund: C. W. K. Gleerup, 1974.

Aulén, Gustaf. *Jesus in Contemporary Historical Research.* Philadelphia: Fortress Press, 1976.

Westerholm, S. *Jesus and Scribal Authority.* Lund: C. W. K. Gleerup, 1978.

Holmberg, B. *Paul and Power.* Lund: C. W. K. Gleerup, 1978.